THE CULTURE EQUATION

Seven Investments that Build Organizations Worth Staying For

DR. RENEE THORNTON

Copyright © 2026
DR. RENEE THORNTON
THE CULTURE EQUATION
*Seven Investments that Build Organizations
Worth Staying For*
All rights reserved.

No part of this publication may be reproduced, distributed, or transmitted in any form or by any means, including photocopying, recording, or other electronic or mechanical methods, without the prior written permission of the author, except in the case of brief quotations embodied in critical reviews and certain other non-commercial uses permitted by copyright law.

DR. RENEE THORNTON

Printed Worldwide
First Printing 2026
First Edition 2026

ISBN: 979-8-9948341-1-4

10 9 8 7 6 5 4 3 2 1

Edited by Joseph Courtemanche

Interior Book Design by Walt's Book Design
www.waltsbookdesign.com

Cover Design by Anna Perotti
By the Sky Design

THE CULTURE
EQUATION

TO THE FAB 5

Before there was data, there was faith.

Before there was a roadmap, there were five leaders who looked at an unproven model, an ambitious vision, and a mission they recognized as their own – and said *yes* anyway.

They didn't wait for certainty. They stepped in when the work was still becoming what it was always meant to be. And because they did, the mission-critical field now has something it has never had before: proof. $3.2 million in documented savings. A validated framework. An evidence-based foundation that will outlast all of us and change how this work gets done for generations of leaders still to come.

This book exists because of their courage. The leaders who will use it to build something extraordinary owe a debt they will never know they carry.

I do.

To the Fab 5 – who dug in before the data existed – your faith didn't just make this possible. It made it real.

This is for you.

TABLE OF CONTENTS

THE 100

I almost quit this work.

Not in the way people say they almost quit and mean they had a hard week. I mean I sat down at my desk on a Tuesday in October 2022, closed my laptop, and walked away from everything I had spent the better part of a decade building.

Let me tell you what happened.

For years, I had been traveling into mission-critical organizations — dispatch centers, law enforcement agencies, fire departments — carrying a message about culture. Specifically, about the connection between the wellness of the people doing this work and the health of the organizations they held together. I had built something called Navigating Adversity — a practical, evidence-based toolkit that gave mission-critical professionals real skills for real pressure. I believed in it the way you believe in something you watched change people's lives.

I scheduled meetings. I showed up. I made the case — meeting after meeting after meeting, in conference rooms and over video calls, in offices where plaques about service lined the walls and the coffee was always burnt.

And I heard the same things, over and over.

"We care about wellness. Absolutely."

"Our people are our greatest asset."

"We'd love to do something about this."

But very few of them did anything. They talked about wellness the way organizations talk about everything they intend to prioritize and never actually fund. EAP numbers got distributed. Posters went up. The real investment — the kind that treats wellness as cultural infrastructure instead of a compliance checkbox — never materialized. Prevention isn't sexy, I was told, more than once. And it isn't cheap.

That I could understand. Budget battles are real. Institutional inertia is real. I had patience for all of it.

What I didn't have patience for — what I couldn't make sense of — was the no-shows.

Leaders would make appointments with me. Confirm them. And then simply not show up. No email. No call. No reschedule. Just silence. The first few times, I assumed something had come up — a staffing crisis, a personnel issue, the thousand fires that mission-critical leaders manage daily. I rescheduled. I followed up. I gave the benefit of every doubt.

But it kept happening. So often that I did something I don't recommend as a coping strategy but couldn't seem to stop myself from doing.

I started counting.

That October, sitting at my desk on a Tuesday afternoon, I stared into the black zoom screen and sighed. I'd been stood up again. I scratched out the 99 in my running tally and replaced it with 100.

One hundred no-show appointments.

I sat with that for a long moment. Then I closed my laptop, stood up, and walked away.

I spent the next few months in something that felt like recovery — though I wouldn't have called it that at the time. I prayed. I thought. I had the kind of honest conversations with myself that are easier to avoid when you're busy enough to never be quiet. I asked hard questions about whether the work still mattered, whether I was carrying it to people who were capable of receiving it, whether there was a different way.

One night, I woke up with something that felt less like an idea and more like a direction.

I had been building a culture change roadmap for nearly a decade. The research was done. The methodology was sound. It was time to find the leaders who were actually willing to do the work.

Not the leaders who would fill a meeting slot and disappear.

The leaders who understood that their culture was costing them something — and were ready to stop paying for the culture they had and start building the one they wanted.

I went looking for them.

The first thing I asked those leaders to do was something simple and terrifying: let their people speak.

I introduced what I now call the Current State Assessment — seven culture markers, measured anonymously, translated into financial terms. Peer trust. Supervisor trust. Leadership trust. Workplace wellbeing. Individual wellness. Culture fit. Whether employees promoted the agency or detracted potential candidates from it. Not a feelings survey. A financial audit of what culture was already costing their agencies, expressed in the language of budgets and bottom lines.

What came back was honest in the way that anonymous data always is — the kind of honesty that had never been safe to say out loud. Depression indicators. Turnover rates that were bleeding agencies dry. Workers who were physically present and psychologically gone.

The leaders who stayed with the process after seeing those numbers weren't the ones who were surprised by them. They were the ones who finally had words for what they'd been sensing for years.

And then I brought them to Mackinac Island.

If you've never been, picture an island that stopped somewhere around 1880 and never resumed. No cars. Horses, buggies, bicycles, and walking. The Inn at Stonecliffe on the west end of the island, away from the tourists. Fall air. Leaves changing. The particular quiet that descends when you've put enough water between yourself and your inbox that your nervous system finally believes you might actually be somewhere else.

I designed it as a pattern interrupt — a forced separation from the noise that keeps mission-critical leaders from ever doing real internal work. I brought them together not to lecture them about culture, but to replenish them first. Because you cannot build something extraordinary from a state of depletion. And nearly every leader in that room had been running on fumes.

We talked about the generational shift rewriting their workforces. We worked through why discovery — the process of excavating what actually drives you beneath the job title and the role and the institutional identity. We addressed the recruitment and retention crises that were keeping agencies chronically understaffed, and we started mapping real solutions. Not programs. Strategies with sequences.

They left the island different.

Not because I said anything revolutionary. Because for the first time, they had a roadmap and hope. They were now among a cohort of people exactly like them — leaders who understood what it costs to hold together organizations built for life-and-death work, who were carrying the same institutional battles, who had been fighting alone and didn't have to anymore.

After the island, the real work began.

Monthly cohort calls. Agency Why Discoveries that gave each organization a sentence it could actually lead with. Strategic scouting plans built from the psychological profile of the 4% — the small percentage of the population hardwired for mission-critical work — so that leaders stopped hiring whoever applied and started pursuing the candidates who were built for this.

Within months, something was visibly shifting. Recruiting was returning hundreds of applicants where agencies had been begging for four. Retention stabilized. The leaders started calling each other — not just for commiseration, but for strategy, encouragement, and the kind of accountability that doesn't exist when you're fighting alone.

The year-one Current State Assessment results came back. They were remarkably better. Not perfect. Not finished. Better in the specific, measurable ways that matter to a CFO and feel like oxygen to the people doing the work.

That's how Leading High-Performing Cultures was born.

Not from a business plan. From a problem too important to abandon and a methodology strong enough to solve it.

Here is what Leading High-Performing Cultures is — what it actually does, beyond the framework that the rest of this book will lay out.

It is a multi-year, supported journey through culture transformation. I lead a cohort of mission-critical leaders through the 7C+ Framework in sequence, answering the hardest questions and resolving the most difficult challenges together. Not in isolation. Together.

We build strategic scouting pipelines that identify candidates with the psychological profile for mission-critical work before a position is vacant. We design DNA Onboarding that transfers organizational identity to new hires from day one, so they feel the culture before they've learned the systems. We teach leaders how to apply people intelligence to their supervision practices — how to lead across four generations, speak the languages of appreciation and apology that actually land, and develop the multi-generational influence skills the current workforce demands.

We train temperament. We teach influence. We build professional brands. We construct the financial case for culture investment in language that CFOs, city managers, and governing boards already speak — and we help leaders present that case to the people above them who control whether what they're building survives.

We provide assessment data connected to financial bottom lines, and we use it to protect what's being built from the annual budget battle that kills good culture work in agencies every year.

All of it grounded in the Culture Equation — the framework at the center of this book. All of it sequenced, because sequence is what separates investment from expense.

The leaders you'll meet in the chapters that follow came through this journey. Their results are documented. Their stories are real. And the agencies they lead are proof that this isn't theory.

Now I want to ask you something.

You're reading this book for a reason. Maybe you're the director running yourself into the ground and wondering if there's a way out that doesn't require abandoning the standards you've spent your career building. Maybe you're the chief who's watched five engagement initiatives evaporate and is tired of justifying the budget for the next one. Maybe you're a deputy or a commander who doesn't hold the top seat but knows that what's happening on your floor is costing people more than anyone's willing to say out loud.

Whatever brought you here — I need you to know this is not a book I wrote to read from the shelf.

The next cohort of Leading High-Performing Cultures is forming now. A select group of mission-critical leaders, invited to Mackinac Island to begin the work. Not enrolled — invited. Because the cohort we're building isn't made up of whoever registers. It's made up of leaders who are ready. Leaders who have done enough honest assessment to know that what they're building needs more than a seminar or a survey. Leaders who are prepared to go first.

If that's you — if you read the chapters that follow and recognize yourself in the leaders you meet — a new cohort is always forming, and I want to hear from you.

Visit pathfinderresilience.com.

The leaders in this book said yes before they had certainty. Some of them said yes while their agencies were hemorrhaging talent and their own confidence was running low. That yes is the only thing they had in common when they started. It was enough.

What follows is what that yes produced.

INTRODUCTION

What Transformation Actually Looks Like

In 2024, 41% of F Division RCMP's dispatch staff showed diagnosable depression.

The director, Jocelyn James, was running herself into the ground – working every weekend, taking every difficult shift, micromanaging decisions because she couldn't trust anyone else to hold the line. Staff described her as angry. Controlling. Present in body, absent in connection.

The center was bleeding. Turnover crushed them. The people who stayed were surviving, not thriving. Peer trust had eroded to the point where asking for help felt like admitting weakness. New hires absorbed the toxicity within weeks.

This is what cultural crisis looks like. Not dramatic explosions. Slow suffocation.

It also has a price tag.

Every departure cost F Division between $50,000 and $75,000 – the full replacement cascade. Diagnosable depression in 41% of the workforce meant elevated sick leave, increased healthcare utilization, and a presenteeism crisis.

PRESENTEEISM The hidden productivity loss when employees are physically present but mentally disengaged. Bodies at consoles, processing calls, operating well below the capacity the mission demands – without triggering a single alarm on any budget line.

The peer trust deficit meant longer call resolution, more supervisory intervention in routine conflicts, and institutional knowledge that wasn't transferring because people didn't trust each other enough to share it. The director's micromanagement – driven by a trust deficit she didn't know how to fix – created a bottleneck that slowed every decision and exhausted the one person the center couldn't afford to lose.

None of this appeared on a budget line. All of it was costing the agency hundreds of thousands of dollars annually.

Twelve months later, the same center hit an eNPS of +71.4.

eNPS – EMPLOYEE NET PROMOTER SCORE A single-question measurement of workforce loyalty: *How likely are you to recommend this organization as a place to work?* Scored on a 0–10 scale, promoters (9–10) minus detractors (0–6) produces a score from -100 to +100. Above 0 means more advocates than critics. Above +50 is stellar.

That's not good. That's world-class.

Eighty-six percent of staff now report healthy psychological states. One hundred percent trust their supervisors to support their professional growth. Zero – not one – considered leaving in the past year. Staff are actively shutting down gossip instead of joining it. They're requesting development opportunities instead of just clocking hours.

What does "shutting down gossip" look like on a dispatch floor? At F Division, a newer dispatcher started venting about a scheduling decision. A three-year veteran – someone who eighteen months earlier would have piled on – looked at her and said, "I get it. But if you've got a problem with the schedule, talk to the supervisor. Complaining here just makes the shift worse for both of us." The conversation ended. Not because someone was punished. Because the culture shift was building peers who protected the environment the same way they protected each other on a call.

> **SOCIAL CAPITAL** The invisible connective tissue of a high-performing organization – the trust networks, peer relationships, and collaborative instincts that amplify individual performance. When Social Capital is high, people cover for each other, conflicts resolve faster, and the culture begins to police itself. That's what happened at this moment: the culture defending what it had decided was worth building.

Culture policing itself because people have decided what they're building is worth defending.

Here's what one team member said about a colleague named Vanessa:

"Last year, she was quiet and reserved and wouldn't share her opinion. Now that she feels valued, she speaks up and becomes part of the team. We are working hard to treat our people with respect, and she's not the only person who's come out of her shell."

And here's what changed in Director James:

She stopped creating order through control. She started creating order through empowerment. Eighteen months into building a high-performing culture, a staffing crisis hit on a Saturday. In the old culture, Director James would have driven in, taken the console, and white-knuckled through the shift herself. This time, her supervisor on duty assessed the situation, reassigned positions, brought in a part-timer, and resolved the gap – all without calling the director. When James saw the incident log Monday morning, there was nothing to fix. Her team had handled it because she'd spent months building them to handle it. She didn't feel relieved. She felt proud.

Her personal why statement — *"I create order from chaos so that the people I care about never lose hope"* — didn't change. But how she lived it transformed completely.

WHY STATEMENT The precise articulation of a leader's core driving motivation — the reason they do this work that persists regardless of role, rank, or organization. A why statement isn't a slogan. It's a compass. When a leader can name her purpose with that level of specificity, it changes how she leads — and it changes how her team understands her.

She let go of weekends. She delegated decisions. She asked staff about their futures instead of just managing their present. She didn't stop being the model of excellence. She chose to another dimension to it by building excellence in others.

Staff now describe her as "phenomenal." One wrote: "I sometimes want to run up and hug her and say thanks for being encouraging when I needed it most."

This didn't happen because F Division got lucky with a hire. It didn't happen because the RCMP suddenly flooded them with resources. It didn't happen because someone gave a motivational speech or hung a poster about values.

It happened because leadership invested in culture the way you'd invest in any critical system — strategically, sequentially, over time.

It happened because someone finally treated culture as a capital project instead of a program.

It happened because the director acknowledged that what she'd been doing wasn't working any longer, then pursued something better. For herself and her team.

And the returns were measurable – not just in the human terms that fill the paragraphs above, but in the financial terms that justify the investment to the people who approve budgets.

In a high-performing environment, a new hire's first impression isn't the complaint culture of the break room. It's the trainer who starts day one by sharing her own why statement. It's the peer who stops by the console during week two to say, "You handled that difficult caller really well. Your tone never shifted." It's the supervisor who checks in at the thirty-day mark not to evaluate performance, but to ask: "What's one thing we could do better for you?" By day sixty, the new hire isn't absorbing culture passively. She's contributing to it – because the culture made clear from the start that her voice was expected, not just tolerated.

Zero turnover in a center that was hemorrhaging talent means avoided replacement costs that run well into six figures annually. Seven hundred applications in an industry where agencies beg for candidates means the cost of recruitment dropped to nearly nothing – the culture does the recruiting. Depression indicators cut by more than half means reduced healthcare claims, lower absenteeism, and a workforce operating at capacity instead of surviving on fumes. One hundred percent supervisor trust means decisions flow without bottlenecks, conflicts resolve at the lowest level, and the director no longer has to be the single point of failure for every operational question.

Every one of those outcomes has a dollar value. And every one of those dollar values was created by strategic investment in culture – not by throwing money at programs that depreciate the moment the applause stops.

Workforce culture is a driving force behind employee intentions, which is exactly why culture has become the term de jour on LinkedIn and at conferences all over the globe. The problem is that it's a buzz word. Something we point to as both the problem and the solution without ever really understanding it.

In the pages that follow, I'll introduce you to the 7C+ Framework. This concept was developed over twenty years while researching organizational interventions. The model is an amalgamation of business, leadership, psychological, financial, and anthropological evidence. In 2024, it was ready to test. This isn't a theory. It's methodology.

The framework operates across seven years and five phases – a construction sequence designed to compound long after the early results are visible. What you're reading documents Phase 1: the first eighteen months of implementation. These are the early returns of a longer arc. What they grow into as the work matures is the subject of Chapter 3.

This book also does something else that no leadership book in this space has done before. It connects each element of culture to a dollar value – grounded in research from Qualtrics, Gallup, SHRM, the CDC, OSHA, McKinsey, and the behavioral science that links trust, wellbeing, and engagement to measurable financial outcomes. Not because culture is reducible to money. But because the people who approve your budget need to see culture in the language they already speak. And because the leaders who build culture deserve to prove that what they're building has returns as real as any apparatus, any facility, any piece of operational foundation their organization has ever funded.

F Division isn't the only story you'll read. You'll meet a 911 director whose agency was bleeding talent – and who kept pushing against institutional headwinds that would have stopped anyone less committed. You'll meet an RCMP director who faced more resistance than any leader in this book and came out the other side fully staffed with hundreds of applicants per posting. You'll see a thousand-person sheriff's department transformed by a leader who mandated investment in his people during a pandemic and held the line through years of skepticism. You'll learn how a deputy fire chief embedded culture change without positional authority, through nothing but the gravitational pull of consistency. And you'll meet a Rational – a leader who lives in logic and systems – who nearly fled from the discomfort of personal development, then became its most outspoken advocate.

You'll also learn what each of those stories cost. Because culture that can't be quantified is culture that can't be protected. And culture that can't be protected is culture that dies the moment a new leader arrives, a budget crisis hits, or a political wind shifts.

But F Division is where we start. Because if you're reading this book, you're probably where Jocelyn James was eighteen months ago: exhausted, holding everything together through sheer force of will, wondering if there's a way out.

There is. But the path I'm writing about runs through you before it runs through your team.

F Division's culture didn't change because the right program arrived or the right budget opened. It changed because the director changed – and because she did, change created the conditions for an exhausted, depressed workforce to become something it hadn't been in years: capable of more. The dispatcher who breathes through a high-volume shift and reaches for a technique that steadies her: she exists because a leader rebuilt herself first. The veteran who intercepts gossip and redirects it toward accountability: he does that because the culture he inherited became a culture worth defending – built by one person who decided the work was worth doing.

The workforce transformation you're about to read wasn't the primary investment. It was the return on one. The primary investment was in the leader.

You cannot strategically invest in your people until you've invested honestly in yourself. That's not a detour from this work. That's the first phase of it.

The only question is whether you're willing to go first.

A note before we begin…

Before we talk about what fails and what works, there's something you need to know about the language we've been using to capture the uniqueness of – and the challenges faced by the people you're leading.

Many of them have been misdiagnosed. And misunderstood.

When a fifteen-year dispatcher starts calling in sick more often, when a veteran officer stops volunteering for anything, when the captain who used to lead every initiative begins doing exactly the minimum, the system reaches for a familiar explanation. Burnout. Secondary trauma. Compassion fatigue.

Rest and recovery prescribed. Wellness days offered. EAP numbers distributed.

But the people you're trying to protect aren't wired the way those prescriptions assume.

THE 4% Approximately four percent of the population is psychologically hardwired for mission-critical work. They possess specific psychological skills – elevated sensation-seeking, hardiness under stress, internal locus of control, discomfort with equilibrium – that can't be taught. These are default wiring, not learned behaviors. Your dispatchers, firefighters, officers, and paramedics who thrive under pressure aren't just trained well. They're built differently. The remaining 96% can do many jobs competently. They cannot sustain the psychological demands of yours.

The 4% aren't wired for equilibrium. They're wired for intensity, meaning, and challenge. When the work becomes routine, when the culture asks them to shrink instead of grow, when leadership stops developing them – they don't burn out. They shut down.

It looks like burnout. It feels like burnout. Every symptom matches. But the condition is completely different entirely.

UNDERSTIMULATION – THE MISDIAGNOSIS The condition where mission-critical professionals are incorrectly diagnosed as burned out when they're actually suffering from insufficient challenge, meaning, or autonomy. Burnout results from being depleted. Understimulation results from being underused. The symptoms are nearly identical. The treatment is opposite: not rest and recovery, but meaningful challenge and investment. Not a wellness day, but something worth fighting for.

You can't build a high-performing culture by treating understimulation like exhaustion. The people who need to be challenged most are the ones most likely to be handed a pamphlet instead – which is one of the reasons so few of them ever admit they're struggling.

This book provides a preview of the cultural frameworks, but don't lose sight of the 4% those frameworks were designed for.

CHAPTER 1

WHY EVERYTHING ELSE FAILS

The transformation at F Division didn't happen because Jocelyn James attended a leadership seminar.

It didn't happen because someone gave an inspiring speech about culture. It didn't happen because HR rolled out a new engagement initiative. It didn't happen because the RCMP suddenly increased their budget, offered sign-on bonuses, or loosened their policies.

Those interventions exist everywhere. And everywhere, they fail.

F Division transformed because someone finally approached culture the way you would any mission-critical system: as a capital project, not a program.

CAPITAL INVESTMENT VS. PROGRAM A capital investment allocates resources to build assets that appreciate over time and generate ongoing returns. A leader developed today develops other leaders for years. A program is a one-time expenditure that depreciates immediately. Motivational speakers come, leave, and the uplifting feeling evaporates. Culture has been treated as a program when it should be treated as capital. Programs create moments. Capital investments create assets. The distinction is the difference between inspiration that fades by Wednesday and a leadership shift that compounds for years.

That distinction – between programs and capital investment – is why you're still struggling with the same problems you had three years ago.

The Intervention Graveyard

You've tried things. Of course you have.

You raised pay. Competitors matched it within months, and the people who were leaving for money kept leaving – because money was never the real problem.

You improved benefits. Those became table stakes. Now everyone offers the same package, and you're back to competing on something you still can't articulate.

You bought new equipment. Necessary. It didn't change how people felt when they showed up for their shift.

You sent people to training. They came back energized for seventy-two hours, then the environment absorbed them back into the same patterns.

You conducted engagement surveys. You have binders full of data. The data told you things you already knew. Nothing changed because knowing isn't the same as building.

You tried pizza parties, appreciation weeks, and motivational speakers. Staff smiled politely. Morale didn't move.

None of these are bad ideas. They're incomplete ideas. And the gap between incomplete and intentional is where your budget disappears.

That pay raise you gave three years ago? If you increased twenty employees by $5,000 each, that's $100,000 annually – recurring, compounding with benefits – and it didn't move the needle on a single departure. The training conference you sent four supervisors to last year? $8,000 in registration, $6,000 in travel, $4,000 in overtime to cover their shifts – $18,000 for seventy-two hours of enthusiasm that evaporated by the following Wednesday. The engagement survey you commissioned? $10,000 to

$25,000 for data that confirmed what your newest hire could have told you on day three.

Add it up. Most agencies are spending $150,000 to $300,000 annually on culture-adjacent interventions that produce no measurable return. Not because the money was wasted on bad things – but because it was spent on disconnected things. Programs without architecture. Investments without sequence. Spending without strategy. Processes over people.

> **CULTURAL WASTE** Money your organization is already spending that produces no return because of cultural dysfunction. The overtime driven by vacancies caused by turnover caused by broken supervisor trust. The recruitment costs inflated by a negative eNPS. The training investment was lost when a new hire leaves in year one. You are already paying for culture. The question is whether you're paying for the culture you want – or paying the consequences of the one you have.

Here's what makes this especially costly: every failed intervention doesn't just drain money. It drains credibility. Every initiative that stalls, fades, or gets absorbed back into the same patterns leaves a residue of skepticism in your workforce. Staff who have watched five engagement initiatives come and go aren't just disengaged – they're immunized against the next one. You start each attempt with less runway than the one before, because the people you most need to reach have learned, from experience, not to believe it will last.

You're not just paying for what didn't work. You're paying interest on it.

Every one of these interventions treats culture as something you can purchase or program – add the right ingredient, and the recipe works. But culture isn't a recipe. It's an ecosystem. And you can't fix an ecosystem with spot treatments.

Compare that $18,000 conference to the same amount invested in Leadership Capital.

LEADERSHIP CAPITAL The foundation of the 7C+ Framework. This is where you develop the leaders who will drive and sustain everything that follows – not management training, but the internal work that transforms how a leader shows up, makes decisions, and develops others. Nothing else holds without it. Every other capital investment you make is only as strong as the leadership underneath it.

An EMS chief completes why discovery and applies her brand to new relationship-building techniques built for the four distinct generations represented on her team. She returns to her department and, within the first week, changes how she opens her Monday briefings. Instead of operational updates and complaints, she starts with one recognition of a team member who modeled excellence that week. Within six weeks, her supervisors begin mirroring the behavior unprompted. Within three months, staff recognize each other without being asked. The chief didn't give a speech about culture. She changed one behavior, and the investment compounded through every person who watched her do it. That $18,000 is still producing returns eighteen months later. The conference stopped producing returns on Wednesday.

The difference isn't the dollar amount. It's the architecture behind it. She put people before processes.

The Real Enemy

Here's what no one tells you about leading mission-critical culture transformation:

You're not just building something. You're fighting something.

You're fighting HR policies designed for corporate environments where the stakes are quarterly earnings, not life and death. You're fighting decision-makers who've never worked a shift where someone's survival depended on their focus. You're fighting institutional inertia that treats your 4% workforce the same as the 96% who clock in, clock out, and never carry the weight your people carry. You're fighting the comfort of the way things have always been done.

And you're doing all of this while also running operations. While managing personnel crises. While attending budget meetings where you're asked to justify expenses in language that was never designed to capture what you're building.

The policies that govern your organization weren't built for you. They were built for environments where "toxic employee" means someone who's unpleasant in meetings — not someone who's actively destroying the psychological safety of people who handle crisis calls for twelve hours straight.

When you try to remove an energy vampire who's poisoning your culture, status quo policies require documentation that would take six months to compile while the damage compounds daily.

ENERGY VAMPIRE / CULTURAL CATALYST Every culture has both. An energy vampire is the team member whose persistent negativity, resistance, or toxicity actively erodes the cultural health of those around them. This isn't a personality conflict. It's a person who creates a ceiling on how far your culture can rise. Staff know exactly who they are. Leadership usually does too. The question is whether anyone has the institutional support to act.

The inverse is equally real. A cultural catalyst is the team member who, when a new hire makes a mistake on a live call, walks over during the next break and says, "Your instincts were right. Here's the one piece you were missing." That interaction takes forty-five seconds. It converts a potential confidence collapse into acceleration. Energy vampires erode. Cultural catalysts compound.

When you try to protect your team from a supervisor who runs to the union every time he's held accountable, you're told to "follow the process" – a process designed for environments where the cost of delay is inconvenience, not trauma.

That six-month documentation process has a price. While you compile paperwork, the energy vampire drives out two good employees. That's two full replacement cycles – recruitment, background checks, academy, field training, overtime to cover the vacancies – to protect the employment of one person who's destroying what you're trying to build. The supervisor who runs to the union? Every grievance he files costs administrative time, legal review, and leadership attention diverted from the mission. Multiply that across a year and the institutional cost of protecting one toxic employee often exceeds what it would cost to invest in five high performers.

The system doesn't just fail your culture. It subsidizes the people who are killing it.

The leaders challenging the status quo aren't failing. They're fighting a two-front war: building culture below while battling for support above. And most of them are fighting alone, absorbing that weight invisibly, because the job description doesn't include a line for the exhaustion of doing the right thing against institutional resistance.

In one agency, the sheriff couldn't remove the energy vampire. So, he isolated the impact. He restructured shifts so the toxic employee had minimal overlap with the newest hires. He assigned the strongest peer mentor to the adjacent workstation. He documented every incident in real time – not for a six-month HR file, but in a running log he could present at any moment. And he created such a strong positive culture around that person that the contrast became undeniable – to the team, to leadership, and eventually to the energy vampire herself, who quit within eight months. Not because she was forced out. Because the culture had become something she didn't recognize and couldn't undermine.

That's not the ideal path. The ideal path is institutional support for timely personnel decisions. But when you don't have the ideal path, you build the culture so strong that toxicity can't survive in it.

The Leaders Who Stayed

The leaders you'll meet in this book represent radically different contexts. A forty-person dispatch center in rural Michigan. A thousand-person sheriff's department serving San Francisco. RCMP communications centres in Canada operating under federal constraints. An emergency services deputy chief in Texas who doesn't hold the top seat. Different sizes, different structures, different institutional challenges.

Same pattern: leaders who stayed when staying was hard. And who changed themselves before they changed anything else.

Consider Caitlin Sampsell.

Director Sampsell runs Berrien County Central Dispatch in Michigan. When she joined Leading High-Performance Cultures, her eNPS sat at -1. More people actively warning others away from the organization than recommending it. She has energy vampires on her team that current policies don't support removing. Her learning edge is delegation – the drive to pursue excellence personally that sometimes means she holds too much herself.

She could have quit the program when it got hard. Other leaders did – leaders who preferred their popularity to the pushback that real change requires. Director Sampsell dug in. You'll read her full story in Chapter 3. What you need to know now is that she kept pushing her agency forward against the kind of institutional resistance that would have broken someone less committed.

Now consider Chris Spence.

Director Spence works for the Royal Canadian Mounted Police running K Division's Operational Communications Centres in Alberta. When he entered Leading High-Performance Cultures, people challenged me for accepting him. They didn't have faith in his leadership. The director he replaced had been a go-along-to-get-along leader. Chris was different. He had grit.

I selected him because I recognized what his stubbornness could produce when pointed in the right direction.

What happened next almost ended his career. Chapter 3 tells that story. For now, understand this: Chris Spence faced more institutional resistance than any leader in this book. He is now fully staffed, with four hundred applicants every time he posts a job opening – in an industry where the average center operates 15% to 25% below authorized strength. That's not luck. That's what happens when a leader refuses to quit.

And consider Paul Miyamoto.

Sheriff Miyamoto leads the San Francisco Sheriff's Office – 993 personnel serving both the City and County of San Francisco. When COVID hit, the culture, by his own staff's assessment, was toxic. An "us versus them" mentality had calcified over years. Trust between frontline staff and leadership had eroded to the point where any initiative from the top was met with suspicion.

In the middle of a pandemic, Miyamoto mandated self-care training for his entire workforce. Not optional. Not suggested. Required. The pushback was immediate and intense. Miyamoto held the line. Four years later, his department achieved the first net-positive retention in a decade.

Chapter 3 tells you how that happened – and what it cost along the way.

The Pattern

All these leaders share something that separates them from the ones who dropped out: they chose the hard road. And they chose it knowing exactly how hard it would get.

They could have optimized for popularity. Culture transformation creates resistance. It surfaces conflict. It requires telling people things they don't want to hear and holding standards that some will never meet. Every leader who starts this work faces a choice: push through the discomfort or retreat to comfortable ineffectiveness.

They pushed through.

One of the fire chiefs who entered this work walked away early – not because the framework didn't work, but because it was working. He'd spent years building a department where he faced almost no resistance. The culture was comfortable. Comfortable for him. When the work began surfacing what was happening beneath that comfort, he made the calculation that his likeability was worth more than his team's transformation. He stepped back before the discomfort could produce anything.

A different leader – charismatic, widely admired – left for a different reason. Not fear of discomfort, but unwillingness to see. When offered a resource that could meaningfully support a young firefighter struggling to balance career, marriage, parenthood, and financial pressure, he declined it flatly. "He needs to man up," he said. "In my day…"

There was no curiosity about what the younger generation was carrying. No appetite to understand what leading across generations actually requires. Just a closed door, dressed up as experience.

Culture change isn't for leaders who long for days gone by. It's for leaders who are ready to do things better than were done for them.

The leaders still standing didn't avoid their learning edges. They worked them in public, in front of their teams, which is the only way learning edges become genuine growth. Director Sampsell is learning to delegate – to trust others with excellence instead of modeling it alone. Director Spence is learning to navigate political capital – to build the organizational relationships that might eventually give him the cover to make hard personnel decisions. Sheriff Miyamoto is learning to translate mandated compliance into genuine culture change – to move from "required to attend" to "choosing to stay."

These aren't weaknesses to hide. They're the growth edges that emerge when you do the work. Leaders who never try never discover their edges. Leaders who quit at the first resistance never develop past them.

The leaders still standing are the ones who decided that building something extraordinary was worth the fight – and who understood that the fight began with themselves. They are the leaders this book was written for.

THE 1% OF THE 4% Within the four percent hardwired for mission-critical work, a smaller subset pursues excellence at the level of cultural leadership. They're not satisfied with surviving their environment. They want to transform it. They see what their organization could become and they're willing to fight to build it. These are the leaders this book is written for.

The System Gap

Even committed leaders with the right framework will struggle if the organizational structure above them doesn't support mission-critical culture.

Policies designed for the 96% create friction for the 4%. Decision-makers who've never experienced mission-critical work don't intuitively grasp why "follow the normal process" isn't adequate when the process takes six months and the damage happens in six days. Institutional systems optimize for liability protection over cultural health – and they treat every environment the same, regardless of stakes.

This institutional mismatch has a financial signature. When the process to address a toxic employee takes months, the real cost isn't the documentation paperwork. It's the high performers who leave during that time because they're tired of watching the organization tolerate what everyone knows is unacceptable.

Research shows that a single toxic employee can drive out multiple good ones – meaning for every energy vampire you can't remove, you're likely losing people you can't afford to replace. When the institutional system can't distinguish between a personality conflict and cultural destruction, the cost of that blindness is measured in vacancies, overtime, recruitment cycles, and the slow erosion of the reputation that makes future hiring possible.

This is why Political Capital – one of the seven capitals in the framework – isn't optional. It's existential.

> **POLITICAL CAPITAL** The relationships with boards, councils, unions, and organizational leadership that provide cover for the hard decisions culture transformation requires. Political Capital means educating stakeholders above you about why your environment is different, documenting results in language that budget-makers understand, and building a reputation that precedes you. Without it, you're fighting alone. The average tenure of mission-critical executives is five years. Political Capital is what ensures that what you build survives after your nameplate comes off the door.

Without political capital, you're fighting alone. You might win individual battles through sheer force of will. But you won't win the war.

The Capital Reframe

Here's what needs to be understood about culture:

It's not soft. It's not unmeasurable. It's not beyond strategic intervention.

Culture is the operating system your organization runs on. It requires capital investment – the same discipline, the same long-term thinking, the same commitment to measurable returns that you'd apply to any mission-critical system.

When your CFO asks for ROI on a new apparatus, you have an answer. When they ask for ROI on your culture initiatives, you go silent – or you mumble something about engagement and hope they don't press.

That silence reveals the problem. Culture has never been treated as capital. It's been treated as overhead – nice to have, hard to justify, first to cut when budgets tighten. Especially when it's been lumped in with training.

But imagine walking into that budget meeting with different ammunition.

You say: Last year, we lost eight employees. At $75,000 per replacement, that's $600,000. Our eNPS was negative, which means our own people were making it harder to recruit, extending our average time-to-fill by forty-five days per position. At $350 per day in overtime to cover each vacancy, that's another $125,000. Our sick leave utilization was 30% above the industry benchmark, driven by a workplace wellbeing score that tells us people are stressed, disengaged, and physically breaking down. Conservative estimate on excess healthcare and absenteeism costs: $80,000.

Then you say: That's $805,000 in cultural waste. Not projected. Not theoretical. Documented from our own data. The culture investment I'm proposing costs a fraction of what we're already losing. I'm not asking you to spend new money. I'm asking you to redirect money we're already burning.

That's a different conversation. That's a conversation a CFO can engage with, a city manager can defend, and a board member can vote for.

But you can't have that conversation until you've measured what culture is costing you. That's what the Current State Assessment does – it captures seven markers of organizational health, each with a documented connection to financial outcomes. Peer trust. Supervisor trust. Leadership trust.

Workplace wellbeing. eNPS. Individual wellness. Culture fit. Seven markers. Seven cost centers. Seven opportunities to translate what feels unmeasurable into what's undeniably quantifiable.

This book will show you how each of those markers connects to dollars – not through speculation, but through industry-standard research from organizations your CFO already trusts: Qualtrics, Gallup, SHRM, OSHA, the CDC, McKinsey. The financial case for culture isn't built on feelings. It's built on the same evidentiary standards you'd apply to any capital expenditure.

The financial difference is stark. A $15,000 motivational speaker creates a moment that's gone in a week. That same $15K invested in leadership development creates a leader who develops other leaders for years. The first is an expense. The second is an asset that compounds.

Your CFO understands compounding. Use that language.

The organizations that figure this out will outperform everyone else. The organizations that don't will keep wondering why their interventions aren't working – and keep spending on the answer without ever getting closer to it.

What Jocelyn James Had That Others Didn't

F Division's transformation wasn't handed to Director James on favorable terms. It was fought for, nearly lost, and salvaged through evidence.

She started with something precious: belief from above. Her direct supervisor, Devin, supported her commitment to culture change. And Rhonda Blackmore – her boss's boss – believed in her enough to dedicate investment resources to the endeavor. That initial support gave Director James runway to build.

Then, partway through year one, Rhonda was sidelined.

Suddenly, Director James was operating without the financial backing that had made the work possible. The institutional support she'd counted on evaporated. She faced the same choice every leader in this position faces: retreat to what's fundable, or find another way forward.

She found another way.

She took the data we'd been collecting — the outcomes that were already emerging — and turned them into ammunition. Zero new hire losses. More than seven hundred applications. Staff are demonstrably happier and healthier than they'd been twelve months prior.

She used that evidence to challenge the status quo. Not by attacking the institution, but by proving that investment in culture produces returns the institution cares about. Recruitment costs. Retention rates. Operational readiness. The language of budgets.

This is what Financial Capital looks like in practice.

FINANCIAL CAPITAL The economic backbone of culture transformation — budget protection, resource allocation, and ROI documentation. Financial Capital isn't just about having money. It's about having money that's protected from the annual budget battle, allocated strategically, and justified with proof. Culture dies without budget protection. And budgets get cut when outcomes aren't documented in language decision-makers understand. Financial Capital is how what you build survives the next leadership transition, the next budget crisis, and the next shift in institutional priorities.

Director James didn't just collect data for a report. She translated outcomes into the specific financial categories that decision-makers above her were already tracking. When her institutional backing disappeared, the numbers were her shield. The RCMP couldn't argue with results documented in their own financial language.

She did the internal work too. She underwent a personal discovery process and faced hard truths about her own patterns – the micromanagement, the control, the belief that only she could handle difficult situations. She changed how she led. She applied people intelligence to her operational excellence. She let go of weekends. She delegated decisions. She moved from creating order through control to creating order through empowerment.

The Current State Assessment didn't sit in a binder. Director James brought the results to her team – not a sanitized summary, but the actual findings. She said, "Here's what you told us. Here's what we're going to do about it. And here's the timeline." Consistently, she reported back: "Here's what we've done. Here's what changed. Here's what's next."

Staff who had filled out a dozen surveys that went nowhere watched their input become the foundation for real change. The next survey had a higher response rate. Not because the survey was better. Because leadership proved that answering it mattered.

The framework gave her a blueprint. Her early support gave her initial runway. When that runway disappeared, her commitment to evidence-based results kept her airborne.

Not every leader gets sustained support from above. But every leader who builds evidence while building culture creates the possibility of earning that support – or surviving without it.

The Question

You're already spending on culture. Every organization is.

Add it up right now. Your turnover replacement costs. Your overtime to cover vacancies. Your recruitment advertising. Your training investment that walks out the door in year one. Your above-benchmark sick leave. Healthcare claims driven by workplace stress. Your productivity loss from disengaged employees who show up but checked out years ago.

That number – the one you've never calculated – is what your culture is costing you today. Not what a culture initiative would cost. What the absence of one is already costing.

The question isn't whether you'll invest. The question is whether you'll invest strategically – in the right types of capital, in the right sequence, with the discipline that transforms intentions into something built to last.

And the harder question: **Are you willing to fight for support from above while you build below?**

Because that's what this work requires. Building culture isn't a one-front war. It's not just about your team, your supervisors, your direct reports. It's about securing the political and financial capital that protects what you build from systems designed to treat you like everyone else.

There's a cohort of leaders who are in that fight right now. Their learning edges are visible because they're actually on the field. They stepped into this experience on faith – faith in the direction, faith in the evidence, faith in each other. Four months in, the internal apathy and resistance their teams initially responded with began to shift. Hope replaced skepticism. These leaders proved to their teams that they were determined to show up for them. They weren't just talking about change. They were doing the hard things that change requires while earning new ways to see the individuals they'd been leading for years.

The leaders who dropped out don't have learning edges. They have excuses.

The 7C+ Framework gives you the blueprint. Seven types of capital. Five phases. Two multipliers. One integrating lens.

But the framework doesn't fight your battles for you. It shows you which battles to fight, in what order, and what victory looks like.

And for the first time, it shows you what each battle is worth – in the financial language that earns you the support to keep fighting.

The next chapter shows you the architecture.

CHAPTER 2

THE ARCHITECTURE

You wouldn't pour the second floor before the foundation set.

You wouldn't install the roof before the walls.

You wouldn't wire the electrical before the framing was complete, then wonder why everything shorted out.

Yet most organizations approach culture with no architecture, no sequence, and no structural integrity. They add initiatives randomly, hoping something sticks. They skip foundational work because it seems too basic. They wonder why everything collapses.

The 7C+ Framework provides what's been missing: a blueprint for cultural transformation that treats the work with the engineering discipline it deserves.

> **THE 7C+ FRAMEWORK** The architecture for cultural transformation introduced in this book. Seven distinct types of capital investment – Leadership, Human, Social, Performance, Professional, Financial, and Political – deployed across five strategic phases, amplified by two force multipliers (+Fun and +Artifacts), and calibrated through a multi-generational lens. The "+" represents the multipliers that accelerate every investment.

But a blueprint only matters if you can prove it works.

That's what this chapter is for. Not instruction – not yet. The detailed playbooks for each capital type come in the books that follow. What you need now is the architecture itself: what the seven capitals are, what each one costs when it's missing, how you measure the health of each, and why the sequence is as important as the substance.

Everything in this chapter has a dollar value attached to it. Because the architecture isn't just a better way to think about culture. It's a better way to fund it.

Seven Forms of Capital

Culture isn't one thing. It's seven things — seven distinct types of capital that high-performing organizations require. Each represents a different category of investment. Each produces different returns. And each has a specific place in the construction sequence.

Here's what matters most about each one: not how to build it, but what it costs when it's missing.

Leadership Capital

Leadership Capital is the foundation. Nothing else holds without it.

This is where you develop the leaders who will drive and sustain everything that follows. Not management training — leadership development. The internal work that transforms how a leader shows up, makes decisions, and develops others.

What it costs when it's missing: every other investment you make. The framework that fails because leaders weren't developed enough to implement it. The team-building retreat that buys cynicism instead of cohesion. The recruitment system that finds good candidates and loses them to a supervisor who hasn't done her own work. Leadership Capital is the load-bearing wall. Skip it and the structure looks complete, but it won't hold.

McKinsey's research shows that seventy percent of culture change initiatives fail – and the primary driver is employee resistance rooted in leadership distrust. Every initiative you've tried that stalled, faded, or collapsed after the first ninety days has a Leadership Capital price tag. Add up the direct investment plus the leadership time diverted to manage resistance. That total is the cost of building on an unbuilt foundation.

Leadership Capital work begins with the Resilience Why Discovery process – a structured methodology that helps a leader name the core driving motivation with the precision required for it to function as a compass rather than a slogan. From there, the work expands into personal brand development and a multi-generational influence framework built specifically for the four generations now sharing mission-critical floors. By the end of Phase 1, the executive leader has a named identity, a documented baseline, and a team that has begun to see them differently. The investment is in the leader first. The returns compound through every person that leader develops.

Human Capital

Human Capital is your people – their recruitment, retention, development, and wellbeing.

This is where the pain is most visible. Turnover. Vacancies. Training costs. Overtime to cover empty positions. The constant bleeding that keeps you in reactive mode instead of building mode.

What it costs when it's missing: the most visible number in any agency's budget – even if nobody's tracking it as culture. SHRM puts the replacement cost range at fifty to two hundred percent of annual salary depending on role complexity. The training pipeline in mission-critical work is longer, and the talent pool is thinner than in most industries, which pushes those numbers toward the high end. A corrections agency losing five officers in a year isn't just absorbing five replacement cycles. It's absorbing the overtime spiral, the burnout cascading through whoever's left, and the institutional knowledge that walked out the door.

Every dollar you don't invest in Human Capital shows up as a much larger dollar on somebody's overtime budget.

> **COST PER VACANCY** The total financial impact of an unfilled position, including recruitment, training, overtime coverage, reduced capacity during the learning curve, and administrative burden. In mission-critical fields, this ranges from $50,000 to $150,000 per vacancy depending on role and training pipeline length. This is the anchor number for most cultural waste calculations – the single most important figure in understanding what your culture is already costing you.

Human Capital work is organized around three core programs. The Agency Why Discovery process – introduced in Leadership Capital at the executive level – is deployed here across the broader workforce, connecting individual purpose to organizational identity in a way that drives retention from the first day. DNA Onboarding ensures that connection begins before new hires have ever taken their first call.

> **DNA ONBOARDING** A culture-immersion process designed to transfer organizational identity to new hires from day one. Traditional orientation covers policies, paperwork, and building tours. DNA Onboarding communicates who we are, why we exist, and what it means to belong here. The goal is that a new hire feels the culture before they've learned the systems.

On the recruitment side, the Field Scouting Academy replaces the re-active posture that has left most agencies dependent on whoever happens to apply.

> **FIELD SCOUTING ACADEMY** The program that operational-izes strategic recruitment. Rather than posting openings and screen-ing whoever applies, the Field Scouting Academy teaches leaders to identify and pursue candidates who possess the psychological pro-file for mission-critical work – building relationships with potential candidates long before a position is vacant. Scouting means you know what you're looking for before you need to fill a seat.

Development of the Agency Intelligence Platform also begins in Phase 1. This is a proprietary, agency-specific tool that takes approximately one year to build and is launched in Phase 2. It functions across multiple capitals – supporting candidate identification, internal communication, self-care delivery, and professional development – and includes lifetime Navigating Adversity licensing for every agency that builds it.

This is the one deliverable that no competitor can replicate, because it is built entirely from your agency's own data, culture, and identity. At Phase 5 graduation, the platform integrates the culture assessment architecture so the agency can conduct its own ongoing research independently.

Social Capital

Social Capital is the invisible connective tissue – trust networks, peer relationships, collaborative systems that amplify individual performance.

When Social Capital is high, conflicts resolve faster. Information flows without hoarding. People cover for each other when it matters. New hires integrate quickly because the existing team actively welcomes them.

When Social Capital is low, every interaction carries friction. Gossip spreads faster than information. Silos form. People protect themselves rather than supporting each other.

What it costs when it's missing: Paul Zak's neuroscience research, published in Harvard Business Review, quantified it directly. Organizations with low trust experience seventy-four percent more stress, fifty percent lower productivity, and thirteen percent more sick days than high-trust organizations. In mission-critical work, the cost compounds through a channel most agencies don't connect to culture: operational safety.

Communication failures between peers drive response errors, workaround behaviors, and incident rates that show up as workers' comp claims and OSHA recordables. Add in the overtime generated by interpersonal conflict – shift swap refusals, sick calls driven by interpersonal avoidance, supervisors mediating disputes instead of leading operations – and the price of low Social Capital becomes one of the largest hidden line items in any agency's budget.

Social Capital must be built before performance standards are introduced. This sequencing isn't intuitive – the instinct is to establish expectations first, then build relationships. But Qualtrics Employee Trends research documents what happens when that order is reversed. Their 2024 data shows that thirty-nine percent of employees with less than six months of tenure plan to leave within twelve months. Their 2025 data reveal a twenty-seven-point intent-to-stay gap between new hires and tenured employees. New hires don't absorb standards in a vacuum. They absorb them through the people around them. If the trust environment is broken when they arrive, performance expectations land in hostile soil – and the investment in recruitment and onboarding walks out the door before it has time to compound.

PSYCHOLOGICAL SAFETY The shared belief that the team environment is safe for interpersonal risk-taking. Speaking up about a concern. Admitting a mistake. Raising a challenge to someone with more rank. Psychological safety doesn't mean avoiding hard conversations. It means people trust that hard conversations won't be weaponized against them.

Social Capital work is built through Leading High-Performing Teams: The Art of Applied People Intelligence – a program designed specifically for the interpersonal dynamics, generational tensions, and trust deficits that are endemic to mission-critical environments. It gives teams the language and practical skills to build horizontal trust intentionally rather than hoping it develops organically.

The Mastermind cohort peer network deepens here as well: leaders stop fighting their institutional battles in isolation and start learning from a cohort of peers facing identical challenges in different agencies. By the end of Phase 2, the culture has developed the connective tissue that no personnel policy could manufacture.

Performance Capital

Performance Capital is your systems, standards, and accountability structure for personal excellence.

Culture without standards is chaos with a mission statement. Values on a poster mean nothing if behaviors aren't defined, measured, and reinforced. Performance Capital creates the operational backbone that turns aspirations into expectations and expectations into results.

What it costs when it's missing: productivity variance that most agencies never measure. Gallup's data shows that disengaged employees cost their organizations eighteen to thirty-four percent of their annual salary in lost productivity. In a department of fifty, even a fifteen percent disengagement rate means seven or eight people operating at a fraction of their capacity – and the people carrying them are the ones most likely to leave. Inconsistent accountability also generates grievances, and grievances generate legal exposure: investigation time, settlements, attorney fees, all of it invisible until the invoice arrives.

Clear standards don't just improve performance. They stop the silent bleed of people doing the minimum because nobody defined the maximum.

Performance Capital work introduces two tools that define what operating at the 4% level looks like in practice. The Navigating Adversity self-care toolkit enters here – not as a wellness program administered to the team, but as an excellence standard the executive visibly models. When the leader practices it openly on the floor, it becomes an expectation of what performing at this level requires, not an accommodation for those struggling to reach it. Career Ladder Mapping follows, giving every team member a visible trajectory of growth with defined milestones – so that the 4% who are psychologically wired for challenge can see exactly what the next level of excellence demands of them. By Phase 3, standards aren't imposed from above. They're owned by the people doing the work.

Professional Capital

Professional Capital is the career journey – visible progression, growing expertise, reputation that precedes people.

This isn't just skills training. It's helping people see their career as a body of work that matters. Where am I going? What am I building toward? Will I be more valuable in five years than I am today?

Staff express this need directly when it's missing:

"There are things I want to learn that don't fit into the job I currently have, but would help prepare me for moving up. I'm not even sure what all I

should be doing to develop myself. I wish I had clarity on how this career should ideally look."

What it costs when it's missing: your best people, first. When someone leaves because they can't see a future, you don't just lose a person. You lose every dollar you invested in building them – and you spend that amount again to replace them. The Center for American Progress puts the cost at twenty-one percent of annual salary for mid-range positions, higher for specialized roles. In mission-critical work, the math is worse because the training pipeline is longer and the talent pool is thinner.

Professional Capital work bridges the internal focus of the first two phases with the external visibility of the final ones. Individual leader branding gives each member of the leadership team a defined professional identity – not a job title, but a reputation that reflects who they are and where they're headed. Agency public narrative development turns that individual work outward, giving the organization a coherent story about what it stands for and who it is built for. Introduced in Phase 2 and deepened throughout Phase 3, Professional Capital is the bridge between building the organism and presenting it to the world.

Financial Capital

Financial Capital is the economic backbone – budget protection, resource allocation, ROI documentation.

Culture dies without budget protection. And budgets get cut when outcomes aren't documented in language decision-makers understand.

What it costs when it's missing: everything else you've built. An agency that invests $500,000 over five years in culture transformation – leadership development, improved recruitment systems, wellness programs, performance standards – and then loses it all in a leadership change hasn't just lost a program. It's lost $500,000 in sunk investment plus the compounding returns those investments were generating. Financial Capital isn't just about having money. It's about having money that's protected from the annual budget battle, allocated strategically, and justified with proof.

A culture budget without ROI documentation is a line item waiting to be slashed. And when it gets slashed, every other capital investment loses its support structure.

Financial Capital work takes the cultural waste documentation that has been accumulating across Phases 1 through 3 and turns it into budget armor. The ROI framework translates every metric – retention improvements, recruitment efficiencies, reduced overtime, lower healthcare claims – into the financial language that CFOs, city managers, and governing boards already speak. A budget protection strategy ensures that what has been built is funded through leadership transitions, economic downturns, and the political shifts that have ended good culture work in agencies across the country. By Phase 4, the investment isn't a line item to be questioned. It's a capital project with documented returns.

Political Capital

Political Capital is how culture survives transitions and influences entire professions.

The average tenure of mission-critical executives is five years. Chiefs come and go. Directors retire. Political winds shift. What happens to everything you built when your nameplate comes off the door?

Political Capital means relationships with boards, councils, unions, and organizational leadership that provide continuity beyond any individual. It means a reputation that precedes you. It means succession planning that ensures whoever comes next understands and commits to the culture that's been built.

What it costs when it's missing: one leadership transition can eliminate everything. If culture produced $300,000 annually in reduced turnover and overtime savings by year five, the real cost of losing it isn't the original investment. It's $300,000 per year for every year the replacement leader takes to rebuild – if they rebuild at all. Political Capital is insurance on every other investment you've made.

Political Capital work culminates in two deliverables that protect the full arc of investment. The stakeholder relationship architecture maps every decision-maker above the executive – boards, councils, unions, city management – and builds a deliberate engagement strategy for each. Succession planning ensures the culture survives the leader who built it, not just the policies she wrote.

The Culture State Presentation – the Phase 3/4 Bridge that gates entry to Phase 4 – is where all of this becomes visible: a formal synthesis of the full engagement's data, delivered first to the Mastermind cohort for refinement, then to the agency's own political stakeholders, with me physically present at every presentation. This is how what you've built gets protected. Not by hoping the next leader cares. By making the results undeniable to the people who outlast any individual.

How Culture Gets Measured

Seven capitals give you the architecture. But architecture without measurement is guesswork with a blueprint.

Here's the problem: most organizations have never calculated what their culture is actually costing them. They track overtime. They track turnover. They don't connect those numbers to their root causes. They keep solving the symptoms and wondering why the disease persists.

The Current State Assessment closes that gap. It measures seven markers across your organization – each one tied to a specific dimension of culture, and each one translatable into dollars. This is what transforms culture from an abstraction into an auditable capital project.

The measurement architecture follows the same two-movement structure as the capital investments themselves. In Movement One – Phases 1 and 2 – measurement is internal only. A pre-launch baseline assessment (M0) is conducted before any work begins, establishing the financial case and the starting point for every metric that follows. Year 1 (M1) and Year 2 (M2) assessments document early returns and guide the work as it develops.

In Movement Two – Phases 3 through 5 – the Agency Partner Perception Assessment is added. For the first time, the agency's culture data is measured not just internally but through the lens of partner agencies: how fire, dispatch, law enforcement, corrections, and community responders experience your culture from the outside. Two external data sets are required before advancing to Phase 4. One tells you where you stand. Two establish a trajectory.

Together, these layers make culture measurable in all directions – not just how your people experience the organization, but how the world beyond your walls sees it.

Here are the seven markers.

Peer Trust measures mutual trust, knowledge transfer, and psychological safety at the horizontal level. When it's low, you see it in safety incidents, communication failures, and workers' comp claims. Those costs are trackable.

PEER TRUST The quality of horizontal relationships across your workforce. When Peer Trust is high, conflicts resolve faster, knowledge transfers naturally, and new hires integrate quickly. When it's low, every interaction carries friction. The dollar cost shows up in operational errors, safety incidents, and the overtime required to manage interpersonal dysfunction.

Supervisor Trust measures whether direct reports feel supported in their growth, receive honest communication, and can raise concerns safely. This is the single strongest predictor of voluntary turnover. Gallup's data confirms that managers account for seventy percent of the variance in team engagement. When Supervisor Trust is low, your turnover problem doesn't have a recruitment solution. It has a leadership development solution.

SUPERVISOR TRUST The quality of the relationship between frontline personnel and their direct supervisors. This is the single strongest predictor of voluntary turnover. People don't leave organizations. They leave supervisors.

Leadership Trust measures integrity, transparency, and confidence in organizational direction. Low Leadership Trust generates what Stephen M.R. Covey identifies as a trust tax – every decision takes longer, every initiative meets resistance, and change efforts fail at McKinsey's documented seventy percent rate. But its inverse is equally powerful.

TRUST TAX The measurable cost imposed on every transaction, communication, and decision in a low-trust environment. High-trust organizations move faster. Low-trust organizations document everything, require approval chains for routine decisions, and meet resistance at every turn. That drag on speed and efficiency has a dollar value.

TRUST DIVIDEND The inverse of the trust tax. The measurable acceleration in speed, efficiency, and performance that high-trust environments produce. Every investment in trust compounds: decisions move faster, conflicts resolve cheaper, talent stays longer, and reputation does the recruiting.

LEADERSHIP TRUST The quality of the relationship between the workforce and executive leadership. Distinct from Supervisor Trust – an employee can trust their sergeant and distrust the chief. When Leadership Trust is low, every initiative encounters resistance. Policies get complied with on paper and undermined in practice.

Workplace Wellbeing measures the environmental quality of the work experience – not the individual, but the organization itself. Purpose, belonging, psychological safety, culture fit. The American Institute of Stress estimates that workplace stress costs employers $300 billion annually nationwide. At the agency level, this marker connects directly to healthcare claims, sick leave, FMLA utilization, and short-term disability – numbers that already exist in your budget.

WORKPLACE WELLBEING The environmental quality of the work experience. This measures the organization, not the individual. Purpose, belonging, psychological safety, culture fit. Workplace Wellbeing is the buffer that protects mission-critical personnel from the cumulative toll of trauma, danger, and stress. When that buffer fails, absenteeism rises, healthcare costs escalate, and operational readiness deteriorates.

eNPS – already defined in the Introduction – carries its full weight here. Research estimates each point increase correlates with approximately $940 per employee in financial growth. When your score is negative, your own people are making it harder to hire.

Individual Wellness measures the personal health status of each team member – physical and mental health, stress levels, coping capacity, feelings of overwhelm, career entrapment. Unlike Workplace Wellbeing, which measures the environment, Individual Wellness assesses the person. The Integrated Benefits Institute estimates presenteeism costs two to three times more than absenteeism and direct medical costs combined. In mission-critical work, a dispatcher or officer operating at diminished capacity isn't just a productivity issue. It's a safety issue.

INDIVIDUAL WELLNESS The personal health status of each team member. Physical and mental health, stress levels, coping capacity, feelings of overwhelm, career entrapment. Unlike Workplace Wellbeing, which measures the environment, Individual Wellness assesses the person. The dollar cost shows up as presenteeism – the invisible productivity drain when people are physically present but mentally depleted.

Culture Fit measures retention intent, tenure patterns, and whether people have actively considered leaving. This is your early warning system. Research shows that roughly fifty percent of employees expressing intent to leave depart within twelve months. Culture Fit lets you see the exodus before it happens – and price the exposure before it hits your budget.

> **CULTURE FIT** The alignment between the individual and the organization. Retention intent, sense of belonging, and whether the person's wiring matches what the mission and culture demand. This is your early warning system – the data that tells you who is already gone in everything but the paperwork.

Together, these seven markers make culture auditable.

When you can measure Peer Trust and trace it to safety costs, when you can measure Supervisor Trust and connect it to turnover spending, when you can measure eNPS and link it to recruitment efficiency – you have something you can take to a budget meeting. You have something a CFO can evaluate. You have something a board can protect.

Imagine walking into that budget meeting with this:

Last year, we lost eight employees. That's $600,000 out the door. Our eNPS was negative, which means our own people were making it harder to recruit, extending our average time-to-fill by forty-five days per position. At $350 per day in overtime to cover each vacancy, that's another $125,000. Our sick leave utilization was 30% above industry benchmark, driven by a workplace wellbeing score that tells us people are stressed, disengaged, and physically breaking down. Conservative estimate on excess healthcare and absenteeism costs: $80,000.

That's $805,000 in cultural waste. Not projected. Not theoretical. Documented from our own data. The culture investment I'm proposing costs a fraction of what we're already losing. I'm not asking you to spend new money. I'm asking you to redirect money we're already burning.

That's a different conversation. That's a conversation a CFO can engage with, a city manager can defend, and a board member can vote for.

The Current State Assessment builds that case. Every chapter that follows connects back to these markers. Every agency story in Chapter 3 was measured through them. And every dollar figure in this book traces to one or more of them.

This is how culture stops being abstract and starts being auditable.

The Force Multipliers

Beyond the seven capitals, two additional elements amplify every investment. These are the "+" in 7C+.

+FUN Strategic, not recreational. People are tired of leaders who take themselves so seriously that work feels like penance. Injecting fun into the transformation process increases engagement, accelerates learning, and makes the hard work sustainable. Leaders who can laugh, celebrate, and enjoy the journey create organizations that people want to belong to. The best indicator of high Social Capital is a team that's safe enough to prank the boss – and a boss secure enough to not just survive it, but compound the culture through it.

+Fun normalizes investment in each other. It creates shared memories that bond teams. And it signals something that no benefits package can: that leadership sees its people as human beings, not headcount filling shifts.

+ARTIFACTS The physical and tangible elements that reinforce a high-performing mindset. Why statements displayed throughout facilities. Visual elements in operational spaces that signal values. Environmental design that supports the behaviors you're building. These aren't decorations. They're reminders. When your values are on the wall, people notice when behavior contradicts them. That's not wall art – it's accountability infrastructure.

Together, these multipliers don't add to the framework – they accelerate it. Every capital investment compounds faster in an environment where people enjoy being part of what's being built and are surrounded by evidence of why it matters.

What It Feels Like to Begin

Leaders who join the LHPC Mastermind experience arrive on Mackinac Island carrying the full weight of their agencies – their vacancies, their energy vampires, their institutional battles, their budgets that never quite cover what the mission requires. They arrive, in many cases, believing they are the only person in their world who sees the problem clearly and cares enough to fight it. And they carry the question that drives them all: *What do I do about it?* That particular loneliness is one of the heaviest things a mission-critical executive carries.

Then they walk into a room full of people exactly like them.

The most common reaction isn't relief. It's a quiet, private moment of wonder: *Do I belong here?*

That moment is one of the healthiest things a leader in this work can experience – because it means they're humble enough to recognize that the room is full of alphas, and that even alphas need each other. The wall doesn't come down immediately. It comes down slowly, in the way that walls between people who've been defending themselves for years always come down: one honest conversation at a time. They start talking. Then listening. Then saying the things they've never said out loud to anyone who would understand.

It's rejuvenating in a way that nothing administrative or operational can touch. Because it reminds them why they came in the first place.

That's the first fire.

There is a moment in nearly every engagement – usually in the first ninety days after the Leading High-Performing Cultures Mastermind event – that no survey captures and no metric predicts. It happens before the data confirms anything. Before the eNPS moves. Before a single new hire stays past day sixty because the culture held them.

It happens when a leader sees their agency's why statement for the first time.

Not the draft. The finished one. The sentence that emerges from the team's Why Discovery process after the questions were asked and the team contributed their stories until a single sentence stopped being a description and became a roadmap. A statement that's equally true and aspirational.

Leaders who have spent careers making rapid-fire decisions – who have run into burning buildings, taken crisis calls at 3 AM, made split-second choices with other people's lives on the line – sit with a single sentence and go quiet.

What crosses their face isn't surprise. It's recognition.

Not just of themselves – though that's part of it. It's recognition of the thread that runs from the person they were on the front lines, fighting the bad guys and pulling people out of wreckage, to the leader sitting in that chair right now. The why statement doesn't tell them something new. It gives language to something they've always known but never had words for. And in that moment, it connects – their individual statement to the agency why their team crafted alongside them. Two expressions of the same purpose. One person. One organization. Same direction.

And then the fire starts to spread.

It doesn't matter whether the conversation is about why discovery, the psychology of the 4%, or the generational fault lines running through their dispatch floors and firehouses. What matters is that the ideas are fresh. Real. Immediately applicable – not theoretical frameworks to be adapted later, but tools they can pick up Monday morning and use on the floor. For a leader who has been handed a hundred programs that depreciated by Wednesday, the experience of encountering something practical – something that gives them a place to put the hope they've been guarding carefully because hope has cost them before – is its own form of transformation.

They leave the island different. Not because they were told to change. Because they caught fire in a room full of people who were already burning.

That fire is what the 7C+ Framework is designed to sustain. The sequence gives it somewhere to go. The capitals give it something to build. And the cohort – the alphas who walked in wondering if they belonged and walked out leaning into each other – keeps it lit through the long middle of the work, when the early wins have settled and the hard building has begun.

This is what the first phase of transformation feels like from the inside.

Not a program rolling out. A person waking up.

Why Sequence Is Non-Negotiable

The most common mistake in culture transformation is doing the right things in the wrong order.

Organizations invest in team cohesion before leaders have earned the trust to guide it. They build professional development programs before performance standards exist to apply them to. They pursue political relationships before they have results worth protecting. In every case, the investment is real. The sequence is wrong. And the return evaporates.

Each misstep has a dollar value. The organization that invested $40,000 in team-building retreats before its leaders had earned credibility? That $40,000 bought cynicism, not cohesion – and now the next legitimate investment starts with a credibility deficit. Building in the wrong order doesn't just waste time. It wastes money and burns the credibility needed to secure future funding. Leaders who try to skip phases don't save time – they guarantee failure at higher cost, because every subsequent investment is building on a foundation that hasn't set.

The five phases of the 7C+ Framework define what gets built when, and why. The sequence is engineering, not preference.

Phase 1 – Internal Foundation (Year 1) builds Leadership Capital and Human Capital. This is where the executive leader does her own work – naming her purpose, building her brand, developing the multi-generational influence skills that mission-critical leadership demands. Alongside that internal transformation, the Human Capital systems take shape: recruitment philosophy, onboarding architecture, retention infrastructure. The Agency Intelligence Platform begins development here. The pre-launch baseline assessment (M0) establishes the financial starting point for every metric and calculation that follows.

Phase 2 – Internal Cohesion (Year 2) builds Social Capital and introduces Professional Capital. The Agency Intelligence Platform launches. With leadership and people systems now in place, the work turns to the horizontal trust networks that determine whether new hires stay or leave – the peer relationships, collaborative systems, and team culture that no policy document can manufacture. Professional Capital is introduced here: leaders begin to develop individual brands, and the agency begins to articulate its public narrative.

Phase 3 – Internal Excellence and External Exposure (Years 3–4) opens with Performance Capital and deepens Professional Capital. Standards are introduced, defined, and owned by the people doing the work. Navigating Adversity enters as an excellence standard modeled from the top. For the first time, culture is measured externally through the Agency Partner Perception Assessment – capturing how partner agencies in fire, dispatch, law enforcement, corrections, and community response experience your organization from the outside. Two external data sets are required before Phase 4 can begin. One tells you where you stand. Two establish a trajectory.

Phase 4 – External Authority (Year 5) builds Financial Capital and Political Capital. Entry to this phase is gated by the Culture State Presentation – a formal synthesis of the full engagement's data delivered first to the LHPC Mastermind cohort for refinement, then to the agency's own political stakeholders, with me physically present at every presentation. Financial Capital turns ROI documentation into budget armor. Political Capital turns documented results into institutional relationships that outlast any individual leader.

Phase 5 – Maintenance and Graduation (Year 6+) closes the engagement. No new capital work is introduced. The agency learns to self-administer ongoing research through the Agency Intelligence Platform, and the culture assessment architecture is integrated so that measurement continues independently after the engagement ends. For leaders whose engagement has ignited rather than satisfied their appetite for this work, the Act 2 / LHPC Master Certification pathway opens – a Certified LHPC Master designation, co-authoring opportunities, and co-presenting at national conferences. This is not an ending. It is the launch point for what comes next.

The sequence cannot be compressed by wanting to. You can only do the work or not do it. And the leaders who do it fully – in order, over time, without shortcuts – build something that no budget crisis, personnel change, or shift in institutional priorities can undo.

What the Architecture Produces

Let me be direct about what this framework produces when you work it fully.

You're building an organization where leaders develop other leaders – not just manage direct reports. Where new hires feel they belong by day thirty, not day three hundred. Where standards are clear, enforced consistently, and owned by the people doing the work. Where careers have visible trajectories. Where peers support each other under pressure instead of protecting themselves. Where evidence justifies investment and political relationships protect what's been built.

You're building something that survives you.

And here's what makes that worth the fight:

COMPOUND RETURNS The accelerating effect of capital investment over time. A leader developed today develops other leaders who develop others. Trust built this year reduces friction for years. Unlike programs, which depreciate immediately, capital investments appreciate. Your CFO understands compounding. Use that language.

An agency that reduces turnover by five positions in year one saves a significant multiple of that investment. In year two, the same culture that retained those five retains five more – plus the institutional knowledge from year one makes new hires more effective, faster. By year three, recruitment costs drop because word of mouth is doing work that job postings used to do. By year five, you're looking at cumulative savings that dwarf the original investment.

Not from any single initiative. From the compounding effect of every capital investment reinforcing the others. *That is the Culture Equation.*

Culture Equation – The premise of this book. Culture is not accidental, aspirational, or abstract. It is the sum of specific, measurable investments made in a specific sequence over a specific period. Like any equation, change the inputs and you change the output. Neglect a variable and the equation breaks. The Culture Equation is the formula for building organizations worth staying for – expressed in the same discipline, the same rigor, and the same financial accountability you'd apply to any capital project. Because that's exactly what it is.

The framework exists. The measurement system exists. The sequence exists.

What's still missing is proof — evidence from real agencies, in real conditions, facing the same institutional headwinds you're facing right now.

That's what Chapter 3 delivers.

CHAPTER 3

THE EVIDENCE

If you've made it this far, you're interested.

But you're also skeptical. You've seen frameworks before. You've heard promises before. You've sat through presentations with impressive-sounding models that evaporated when exposed to reality.

You want proof.

Fair enough. Here it is.

How to Read These Stories

Each story that follows comes in two layers. First, the narrative – what happened, who led it, what it cost them personally. Then the financial translation – what those outcomes are worth in the language your CFO, your board, or your city council already speaks. You need both. The story creates conviction. The numbers create permission to act on it.

I've deliberately varied how the financial translations are structured. Some build from the ground up. Some lead with the biggest number. One is a single paragraph. The data is rigorous in every case. But if the fourth translation read exactly like the first, you'd skim it – and these numbers are too important to skim.

The financial anchor is the replacement cost you encountered in Chapter 2 – $50,000 to $100,000 depending on role. When these stories refer to "a full replacement cycle," that's the number. You already know it. Here's what it looks like in practice.

San Francisco Sheriff's Office: The Long Game

In 2020, Sheriff Paul Miyamoto faced a problem every mission-critical leader recognizes.

His department – 993 personnel serving both the City and County of San Francisco – was fracturing. COVID had isolated an already stressed workforce. The culture, by his own staff's assessment, was toxic. An "us versus them" mentality separated frontline employees from leadership. Trust was low. Morale was lower. The feedback Miyamoto received about organizational culture was, in his words, "largely negative."

He could have waited for conditions to improve. He didn't.

Sheriff Miyamoto became the first mission-critical leader I encountered who mandated self-care training for his entire workforce during a pandemic. Not optional. Not suggested. Required – for all 790 sworn officers and 203 professional staff.

The pushback was immediate.

Concerns about confidentiality. Skepticism that any trainer could understand law enforcement's unique challenges. Resistance to the mandate itself. Questions about whether wellness training was "real" work or a distraction from it.

Miyamoto held the line. He sent department-wide communications explaining his reasoning. He instructed supervisors to create relief schedules so every employee could spend two hours per week on the training. He kept communicating his support even when the resistance continued.

Eventually, 754 employees completed the full Navigating Adversity training for POST credit. Another 82 completed it anonymously. Approximately 25% of those who finished went through the entire course again — on their own time.

Here's what one deputy wrote:

"Initially, I was hesitant to dive into this course because I was worried that someone, somewhere would be able to access my work. What if I got sued on the job? Would my written work, or even the fact that I went through the class, be held against me?… Since then, I've actually been doing extra work in the online classroom. I think I've been through the entire course at least twice and some areas more than that."

The San Francisco Sheriff's Office was nominated for a wellness award based on this work.

But the real evidence came later. Instead of treating the experience as a one-time event, Miyamoto continued investing. He sent more than 300 of his staff through the agency why discovery process, allowing them the opportunity to share what made them the proudest about doing the work and ultimately curating those stories into a single sentiment that now leads every recruitment and retention endeavor:

"We are San Francisco's best kept secret. We prioritize respect, accountability, and trust while creating genuine connections that serve as a catalyst for differentiating us as proud, professional public servants."

For years, the department hemorrhaged new hires. Training someone for months, watching them leave within a year, starting over. The cycle repeated itself until people stopped believing it could change.

Then it changed.

For the first time in a decade, San Francisco Sheriff's Office achieved 45% net positive retention. Not 45% retention – 45% *net positive*. More people are staying than leaving, by a margin that hadn't existed in ten years.

The moment it crossed the line.

Partway through the Navigating Adversity training rollout, something shifted that no metric captured in real time. Deputies who had completed the training started talking about it – not in formal feedback forms, but in briefings, in hallways, between calls. A sergeant mentioned, unprompted, that he'd been using a stress management technique from the training. Three deputies nodded. They'd been doing the same thing. Nobody had coordinated this. Nobody had been asked to report back.

That was the moment. Not the completion rate. Not the nomination. The moment when the training crossed from compliance into conversation – when what had been mandated became what people were choosing to bring to each other. Miyamoto hadn't just changed a policy. He'd changed what people thought was worth talking about on shift.

The culture shift was palpable. Staff described it in terms that don't fit neatly into metrics:

"There is no real way to express in words the change in the air at work. It feels lighter somehow."

"The leaders are more open and expressive about their own struggles, which makes it easier to trust and relate to them."

"The separation felt between the line staff and leadership is fading. There is a shared experience for the whole workforce."

What does "lighter" look like in a thousand-person department? It looks like a shift briefing where a sergeant shares, unprompted, that he's been working on breathwork techniques he learned in the training – and three deputies nod because they've been doing the same thing. It looks like a deputy who would have previously dismissed a peer's struggle now saying, "I've been there. Here's what helped me." It looks like the line between "leadership" and "line staff" blurring – not because rank doesn't matter, but because shared vulnerability created a currency that rank alone never could. The training didn't teach them new skills for the job. It taught them new ways of being human with each other while doing the job.

Sheriff Miyamoto didn't have favorable conditions. He had a toxic culture, a pandemic, institutional resistance, and a thousand-person organization that had learned to distrust leadership promises. He invested anyway.

That's what long-game commitment looks like.

The Dollar Translation

Start with what the department was losing. In a 993-person agency hemorrhaging new hires for a decade, even a conservative estimate of fifteen departures annually generates $1.5 million to $2.25 million in annual replacement costs for sworn officers at this scale. That's before you count overtime to cover empty positions, productivity loss during the learning curve for each replacement, and institutional knowledge that evaporated with every departure.

Now price the turnaround. Forty-five percent net positive retention means the bleeding didn't just slow – it reversed. If the department retained even ten additional personnel annually compared to its pre-intervention baseline, that's roughly $1 million in avoided replacement costs per year. Factor in reduced overtime from fewer vacancies, lower healthcare utilization as wellness improved, and the recruitment efficiency that comes from a department people recommend to colleagues, and the annual financial impact enters seven-figure territory.

The Navigating Adversity training itself – two hours per week per employee – required real operational investment. Relief scheduling for nearly a thousand people isn't free. But the return on that investment compounded every year the retention gains held. By year four, the cumulative savings dwarf the initial cost by a factor that any CFO would recognize as an exceptional return.

F Division RCMP: The Transformation Proof

You already know the headlines. You read them in the Introduction – the eNPS score, the turnover numbers, the application volume, the depression indicators. Those numbers are real, and they're extraordinary.

But numbers obscure as much as they reveal. Here's what those numbers don't tell you.

2024 baseline: 41% of staff showed diagnosable depression. Compassion fatigue was endemic. The director was sleeping an average of three hours a night. Eating like a college student. Running on fumes.

The behavioral changes were visible before the metrics caught up. On a recent Tuesday, a dispatcher used a breathwork technique between calls during a high-volume shift – openly, at her console, without apology or explanation. The dispatcher beside her noticed and said, "Good call. I should do the same." Neither treated it as unusual.

In the old culture, using a wellness tool on the floor would have been mocked as weakness. In the new culture, it's treated as what it is: operational maintenance. The same dispatcher, later that shift, handled a caller in acute distress with a vocal calm that her supervisor later cited as a training example. She wasn't performing calm. She was operating from a baseline that the culture – and the tools the culture provided – had made possible. That's not wellness as a program. That's wellness *woven into how the center operates.*

The moment the culture turned.

The Current State Assessment results came back, and they were hard to read. Director James sat with them for less than twenty-four hours before she made a decision that would define everything that followed.

She had been hurt by some of what her team had said. The feedback was honest in the way that anonymous surveys sometimes are – the kind of honesty that lands differently than a conversation, because it carries the collective weight of people who hadn't felt safe enough to say it out loud. She could have defended herself. She could have contextualized the data or shared a sanitized summary with a plan attached.

She didn't. She brought the full results to her team and stood in front of them without armor. She acknowledged their perception without explaining it away. She said, in effect: I see what you've been experiencing. I'm not going to argue with it. Here's what I'm going to do differently.

In doing that, she created her own pattern interrupt – not the kind that happens on an island, but the kind that happens when a leader chooses vulnerability over self-protection and the room goes quiet because nobody expected it.

> **PATTERN INTERRUPT** Any deliberate disruption of habitual thinking or behavior designed to create space for new patterns to form. Growth requires unfamiliar territory. A pattern interrupt can be a structured experience – like the annual Mastermind on Mackinac Island – or it can be a single moment of unexpected honesty from a leader who decides the old way of operating is no longer acceptable.

The team's response wasn't immediate celebration. It was something quieter and more durable: the beginning of belief. Not belief that everything was fixed. Belief that their director was actually going to try. That distinction – between a leader who acknowledges problems and a leader who makes herself accountable to solving them – is what separates a survey debrief from a culture turning point.

Everything that followed was built on that moment.

Then the institutional support disappeared. Partway through Year One, Rhonda Blackmore – the senior leader who had championed the investment – was sidelined. Suddenly, Director James was operating without the financial backing that had made the work possible.

Her team worried that the work they'd done would have to stop. Then the entire RCMP tightened the purse strings to an extreme level, causing a shockwave of concern that staffing cuts would follow.

Director James refused to accept defeat. She took the data that had already been collected – the outcomes that were already emerging – and turned them into ammunition. She translated results into the specific financial categories that decision-makers above her were already tracking. Recruitment costs down. Overtime decreased. Sick leave improving. The language of budgets.

When her institutional backing disappeared, the numbers were her shield. The RCMP couldn't argue with results documented in their own financial language.

2025 outcomes: Depression indicators dropped from 41% to approximately 15%. Staff didn't just stop leaving. They stopped wanting to leave – zero considered departure in more than twelve months. New hire retention hit 100%. And over seven hundred people applied to work there in an industry where most agencies can't fill a single posting.

Director James dedicated time to learning what she'd never been taught growing up: how to listen and respond to her body's needs. She changed her eating habits, started doing hot yoga, and learned how to control every sleep signal she gave her body. Today she averages seven hours of restorative sleep a night.

The RCMP, like most large institutions, operates on policies designed for the broad workforce. Director James didn't wait for those policies to change. She built the evidence case that might eventually change them – while continuing to transform herself and her culture inside the constraints that existed.

The Dollar Translation

Here it is in a single paragraph. Forty-one percent of staff operating at diminished capacity from diagnosable depression – conservatively a twenty to thirty percent productivity loss per affected employee, compounded by elevated sick leave and overtime coverage – represents a six-figure annual drain before a single person walks out the door. Add four to six departures annually at the replacement cost for dispatchers, and the bleeding exceeds a quarter million. Now reverse it: zero turnover eliminates $200,000 to $450,000 in annual replacement costs. Seven hundred applications eliminate recruitment marketing spend entirely and provide selection power that reduces training washout – each avoided washout saves a full training cycle. Depression dropping to 15% recovers the presenteeism loss, reduces healthcare claims, and cuts the overtime that covered absent staff. The total annual financial impact of this transformation: $300,000 to $600,000 in a single center, compounding every year the gains hold. Director James built this while losing her funding, inside an institution that wasn't designed to support what she was doing.

Bucks County 911: The Conversion

Director John Geib almost left on day one.

Our Leading High-Performance Cultures Mastermind events are hosted on Mackinac Island in Michigan – a location selected strategically. It's an island halted in time. No cars. Horses, buggies, bicycles, walking. The Inn at Stonecliffe sits on the west side of the island, away from town traffic. Our summits come at the end of tourism season when the island is nearly empty. It's chilly. The leaves are changing. It smells like fall. The environment itself is a pattern interrupt – a forced separation from the noise that prevents leaders from doing real internal work.

Then we bring in Rodger, our resident evidence-based practitioner in healing modalities. He's a master at the approaches that modern medicine sometimes underestimates – mindfulness, breathwork, energy healing, group meditation. In true high-performing fashion, I push every cohort leader to try these modalities. Not because I expect them to love it. Because growth happens in discomfort.

John is a Rational on the Keirsey temperament scale.

RATIONAL (KEIRSEY TEMPERAMENT) One of four temperament types in the Keirsey framework, characterized by strategic thinking, systems orientation, and skepticism toward anything that can't be measured. Rationals live in logic and data. They're naturally resistant to approaches that feel intuitive or emotional. Leaders who identify as Rationals often find the personal development dimensions of culture work most challenging – not because they lack depth, but because the modalities feel incompatible with how they're wired. Their transformation, when it happens, tends to be the most dramatic precisely because the distance traveled is greatest.

So am I. Rationals live in logic, strategy, systems. We're skeptical of anything that can't be measured. We're allergic to anything that feels like emotional indulgence.

John was not loving the woo woo.

After the first day, he nearly left. The breathwork felt foreign. The meditation felt pointless. The energy healing felt like nonsense dressed up in mystical language. Everything in him wanted to retreat to the familiar – spreadsheets, metrics, problems he knew how to solve.

Instead of doing what other, less forthright leaders have done – smile politely, participate minimally, dismiss it privately – John told me the truth. He was uncomfortable.

I was deliriously happy.

Discomfort is where growth lives. The 4% spend their careers running toward what others run from. Why should personal development be any different? Seek adversity, I told him. You're built for this.

He stuck with it.

He tried the breathwork again – not because he believed in it, but because he was brave enough to test his own resistance. He sat through the meditation. He let Rodger work with him. He forced himself to embrace the discomfort rather than escape it.

The moment something unexpected arrived.

John didn't leave the island as a convert. He left as something more interesting – a skeptic with a crack in the wall.

What broke through wasn't the breathwork itself. It was the room. Specifically, it was the moment he realized that the other leaders around him – the chiefs and directors who ran operations that dwarfed his, who carried institutional weight he recognized immediately – were asking the same quiet question he was asking himself: *Do I belong here?*

That question, shared without being spoken, was the thing the island was designed to produce. Not certainty. Not comfort. The recognition that even alphas need each other – and that the willingness to sit in discomfort together, in a room where everyone is fighting some version of the same battle, is its own form of strength. John didn't leave transformed. He left believing transformation was possible. That was enough to bring him back.

When John left the island, he had the beginnings of a new man.

He didn't just learn the concepts. He applied them. He started fasting – something the old John would have dismissed as unnecessary suffering. He trained for a 5.7-mile race and ran it at the very next summit. His skepticism had transformed into curiosity, and his curiosity had transformed into commitment.

His team noticed. They followed his lead.

John is now our most outspoken advocate for the healing modalities in LHPC. The Rational who almost fled from breathwork now champions it to other skeptical leaders. When we meet, he shuts down all screens and silences his phone as a show of true leadership presence, then focuses completely on what we're doing. He models the behavior he expects.

But here's where John's transformation becomes something larger than personal development.

We offer all LHPC leaders the option of reaching out if they have staff members who need one-on-one attention. Someone struggling. Someone who might benefit from the kind of intensive, nontraditional support that most organizations can't provide.

John was the only leader who took us up on that offer. So far.

He had a female employee of more than a decade who was struggling. Not a performance problem – a human problem. Someone who had given an entire career to the work and was breaking under the weight of it. Most directors would have referred the employee to EAP, documented the conversation, and moved on. John believes in his team too much for that.

He activated support resources in a way the institution alone couldn't. Rodger and I spent months with this person, one-on-one. The same modalities John had initially resisted became the tools that helped bring healing. A valued member of his team went from feeling unloved to knowing exactly what belonging feels like. Here's how she explained it: *"I don't know how to describe what this has done for me. I feel seen. But more than that, it's the first time I've really felt like I mattered…maybe in my whole life."*

That's what Leadership Capital looks like when it's fully developed. Not just personal transformation – the willingness to extend that transformation to others, to fight for resources that don't fit the standard playbook, to believe in people when believing in them is inconvenient.

Now layer in what John built for his staffing pipeline at Bucks County.

Like every 911 director, he faced the recruitment crisis. Not enough applicants, and the ones who applied often weren't the right fit. The conventional wisdom said recruit young – Gen Z digital natives, Millennials seeking meaning.

John's data told a different story.

When we analyzed differentiators during the Bucks County Why Discovery experience – a process that incorporates the identity of likely source professions for future scouting purposes – a pattern emerged that no one expected. One of the ideal candidates wasn't Gen Z. It wasn't Millennials. It was Gen X women going through divorce.

Think about what that profile represents: people in their forties and fifties, navigating the most difficult transition of their adult lives, looking to prove to themselves they could do something incredibly challenging while reinventing who they were. Resilience was forged through adversity. Motivation beyond a paycheck. Maturity to handle crisis without becoming one. That's not a demographic most recruitment strategies target. John targeted it anyway.

He established relationships with women in newly divorced social groups. Not to recruit directly – to open doors. Strategic scouting replaced desperate hiring. The same willingness to embrace uncomfortable approaches that kept him on Mackinac Island led him to pursue candidates everyone else overlooked.

The results reshaped his applicant pool. But something else happened.

The older employees – veterans who had grown bitter waiting for retirement, disengaged from an organization they'd stopped believing in – started re-engaging. The same generational lens that identified the ideal external candidate revealed what internal veterans needed: recognition that their experience mattered, that their stage of life wasn't a liability, that reinvention was possible inside the organization too.

Staff who had been counting down days until retirement started volunteering for committees. People who hadn't raised their hand in years started contributing ideas. The culture didn't just attract new talent – it reawakened talent that had gone dormant.

The moment a veteran stopped counting down.

One of the veterans who had a countdown to retirement he ticked off daily started using the Navigating Adversity self-care toolkit – and for the first time, heard language for what he'd been experiencing. Not burnout.

Understimulation. He'd spent fifteen years doing work he was overqualified for, with no one asking what he still had to offer.

After one of the monthly workshops, he approached me and said, "I want to mentor some of the newer hires. Nobody showed me how to carry this work when I started. I don't want them to figure it out alone like I did."

Within three months, he was running informal peer coaching sessions on his own time. He retired his daily ticker instead of his career. Not because anyone told him to stay. Because he finally had a reason to.

eNPS at Bucks County: +33. Strong organizational health in an industry where positive scores are rare.

John Geib walked onto Mackinac Island as a skeptic who almost fled from discomfort. He walked off as a leader willing to try anything that might help his people – including modalities he once would have dismissed, candidates he once would have overlooked, and investments in individual employees that most organizations would never make.

John has truly personalized this journey. He didn't just implement a framework – he let it change him. And then he extended that change to everyone around him.

That's what Leadership Capital development looks like.

The Dollar Translation

Start with the biggest number: the employee John invested in personally. If she had left – which, without intervention, was the trajectory – the replacement cost alone would have run a full cycle. But the real cost would have been the signal it sent to every other veteran watching: that years of service doesn't earn you anything beyond an EAP referral. John's investment in one person was also an investment in the retention of everyone who noticed.

Now scale outward. Each disengaged veteran represents a presenteeism cost of eighteen to thirty-four percent of their annual salary, according to Gallup's research. For a fifteen-year dispatcher earning $55,000 to $70,000, that's $10,000 to $24,000 per year in lost productivity – from someone still collecting a full paycheck. Multiply that across even five re-engaged veterans and the annual productivity recovery runs from $50,000 to $120,000. Because these are experienced employees, their re-engagement doesn't require a training investment. The institutional knowledge is already there. It just needed a reason to show up again.

The Gen X recruitment insight changed the economics of the new-hire process going forward. Dispatcher training runs approximately six months at roughly $14,000 in trainee pay alone – before overtime for the trainer, equipment, and supervision hours. Washout rates during training typically run twenty to forty percent, meaning agencies invest that full amount in two to four people for every one who becomes operational. John's targeting of candidates with the psychological profile to succeed – resilience, maturity, intrinsic motivation – reduces washout rates, which means fewer training cycles wasted, faster time to full operational capacity, and a lower effective cost-per-hire.

Estimated annual financial impact: $200,000 to $350,000 in a single center.

Berrien County: The Culture Waiting to Be Built

Before a new dispatcher at Berrien County 911 walks through the door for her first shift, a card arrives at her home. Handwritten. Personal. From a colleague she hasn't met yet.

Nobody mandated this. No budget line funded it. Director Caitlin Sampsell didn't design it.

Six dispatchers did.

They call it Team Connect. Two of them volunteered to form it. They recruited four others. They wrote the onboarding process themselves, presented it to their director, and started running it. On a new hire's first day, welcome signs line the entrance. Her locker has been decorated with a personalized magnet. Her training book includes a staff directory – not an org chart, but names and photos, because in a high-performing culture, people aren't headcount. They're colleagues you recognize on sight.

During her first week, a Team Connect member introduces herself, hands the new hire a directory of the committee – photos, contact information, a personal fun fact for each member – and walks through a get-to-know-you questionnaire. The answers become bulletin board postings and internal newsletters. The rest of the team is encouraged to seek the new hire out not to evaluate her, but to learn what she cares about and what brought her to this work. By the end of week two, the new hire hasn't just been oriented. She's been known.

Each new hire is assigned a Team Connect point person on her shift – someone whose job isn't training but connection. Weekly check-ins. Not performance reviews. Conversations: How are you doing? What's been hard? What do you need? The kind of questions that, in most centers, nobody asks until the exit interview – when it's too late to matter.

Team Connect didn't stop with new hires. They started running the same get-to-know-you process with supervisors and administrative staff, sharing profiles monthly – humanizing the people behind the titles, building the horizontal trust that turns a roster into a team.

This is what Social Capital looks like when it takes root. Not a program handed down from leadership. A culture reproducing itself through the people who've decided what they're building is worth protecting.

Now consider where this happened.

Director Sampsell was leading a center that was bleeding. When she entered Leading High-Performance Cultures, her eNPS sat at -1. More people actively warning others away from the organization than recommending it.

Compassion fatigue – the gradual erosion of empathy and emotional capacity that results from prolonged exposure to others' suffering – was widespread across her floor.

COMPASSION FATIGUE The gradual erosion of empathy, hope, and emotional capacity that results from prolonged exposure to others' suffering. Distinct from burnout, which results from organizational dysfunction. Compassion fatigue doesn't mean they've stopped caring. It means their capacity to care has been depleted without being replenished. In mission-critical environments, it accumulates silently – invisible on any performance metric until the day a veteran who used to give everything starts giving the minimum.

The cultural floor had rotted through in places, and she could feel it beneath her feet every shift.

Eighteen months later: eNPS at +11.1, a twelve-point swing from negative to positive. Supervisor trust at 100%. Staff using self-care tools openly on the floor. New hires reporting, without prompting, that they feel welcomed.

And six dispatchers, on their own initiative, building the infrastructure to make sure that feeling never stops.

The question isn't why the numbers aren't higher. The question is what kind of culture produces Team Connect in the first place – and produces it here, under these conditions.

Because Director Sampsell has an energy vampire on her team. Not a difficult personality – a person whose persistent toxicity creates a ceiling on how far the culture can rise. Her staff knows exactly who it is. She knows. Current policies require months of documentation before any personnel action is possible, while the damage compounds daily. One staff member put it plainly:

"This has been clearly stated numerous times, but our leadership knows that one person is the crux of almost all the issues in morale our team faces, and yet nothing is done about it."

That frustration is real and it's legitimate. The institutional system isn't built for this environment, and the human cost of that gap isn't theoretical.

But here's what happened anyway: two dispatchers looked at that environment – the energy vampire, the institutional headwinds, the eNPS that started in negative territory – and decided none of it was an excuse. They built Team Connect because the culture had already become something worth defending. Not perfect. Not finished. Worth defending.

The moment the culture decided to reproduce itself.

The first handwritten card went out before anyone had a system for it. A Team Connect dispatcher simply thought: someone is about to walk into this building for the first time, and they should know they matter before they get here.

Director Sampsell didn't learn about the card until after it had been sent. That was the moment she knew something had changed. Not because she had built a program. Because her people had built something she hadn't asked for – and they'd built it because the culture had given them a reason to. A new hire who received that card in the mail before her first shift later told her point person: "I didn't know places like this existed." She said it in a center still carrying an energy vampire on the schedule.

That's not a culture waiting for better conditions. That's a culture that has already decided what it is.

Director Sampsell is reinforcing the architecture from her position. She ordered shirts for every staff member – agency name on the front, the team's why statement on the back. She purchased gold frames for the main wall, one for each employee's photo, designed to hold written encouragements and accolades that accumulate over time. Not a static display. A living record of recognition that will grow as the culture grows. These are +Artifacts in practice – the physical evidence of a culture that has decided its people are worth commemorating.

Her staff sees both the effort and the evolution:

"I watch Caitlin. She's always been one of us, but she's also always been too refined somehow – too smart to be anything but our leader. This year she's started stepping into her power and it's been great to watch. It feels good to say I'm actually proud of my boss."

"I've only been on the job a short while, but every step of the process so far – from the interview to my first day on the floor – has given me a true picture of a culture worth staying to help build."

That second quote is the one to hold. A new hire, in a center still carrying real constraints, already using the language of investment: *a culture worth staying to help build.* He didn't learn that from an onboarding checklist. He learned it from six colleagues who showed him what belonging looks like before he'd earned a single performance review.

Director Sampsell is learning to delegate – to trust others with excellence instead of carrying everything herself. It's her growing edge and she's working on it. But the clearest evidence that she's already succeeded at the foundational work? She built a team willing to invest in the culture themselves. The director's role in Team Connect is minimal by design: a heads-up when a hire is coming, a welcome card, a few color pages printed. That's it.

The rest belongs to the floor.

One of the newer team members told her Team Connect point person:

"Nobody's ever done anything like this for me at a job before. I didn't know workplaces could feel like this."

The Dollar Translation

A twelve-point eNPS swing has a price. Research estimates each point increase correlates with approximately $940 per employee in financial growth. Across a twenty-person center, that swing represents roughly $225,000 in projected financial value – already compounding in reduced recruitment friction, improved word-of-mouth, and the accelerating retention gains that follow when new hires feel the culture before they've learned the systems.

But the sharper financial story is what one unaddressed obstacle is costing while everything else builds.

A single toxic employee drives out an average of two good employees per year, according to Harvard Business School research on workplace toxicity. At the replacement cost for dispatchers, that's a six-figure annual drain from driven turnover alone – before you calculate the presenteeism effect on everyone who stays. Gallup's data on disengagement suggests each employee within the toxic person's influence radius operates at eighteen to thirty-four percent reduced productivity. In a small center, that radius is everyone.

The personnel decision that current policy makes difficult isn't a culture decision. It's a financial one – and the cost of delaying it runs to six figures annually.

What Director Sampsell has built – improved supervisor trust, peer-led culture infrastructure, new hires who feel belonging before they've taken their first solo call – are leading indicators. They predict reduced turnover before the turnover numbers fully reflect it. They signal recruitment improvement before the applicant pool visibly shifts. The returns are real and they're growing.

Remove the single constraint that institutional policy currently protects, and the timeline to full transformation compresses dramatically. That's not a hedge. That's the most precise ROI calculation in this book: one personnel decision, six figures annually, and a culture that's already proven it knows what to do with a clean runway.

Estimated current annual impact: $150,000 to $250,000, with significant acceleration the moment institutional barriers are addressed.

K Division RCMP: The Grit Test

Director Chris Spence has the most improbable success story in this book – because he built it while nearly everyone around him tried to tear it down. And he started this journey in his first year as the new director of two centers in Alberta.

When Chris entered Leading High-Performance Cultures, people challenged me for accepting him. They didn't have faith in his leadership skills. The director he replaced had been a go-along-to-get-along leader. Someone who kept the peace by never pushing for change. Chris was different. He had grit. He was stubborn enough to hold the line when holding the line meant standing alone.

I selected him because I recognized what that stubbornness could produce if pointed in the right direction.

I underestimated what he'd have to survive to prove it.

2024 baseline: 31% diagnosable depression. 59% compassion fatigue – more than half of his workforce with their capacity to care actively eroding beneath the surface of every shift. Survey response rate of 33% – people had stopped believing their voices mattered. A culture that had learned to expect nothing and received exactly that.

Then Chris started building. And the resistance started mounting.

The national union president fought against the work he was doing. His own command staff abandoned him – two out of three of his highest-level leaders refused to support him when he continued pushing the LHPC initiative forward. He lost leaders in his above-level chain of command. People in peripheral, peer-level roles – who should have had his back – walked away or actively worked against him.

He was nearly fired for continuing to drive this initiative forward.

Read that again. A director, trying to build a healthier culture for his people, nearly lost his job for refusing to acquiesce to the way it's always been.

Most leaders would have folded. The institutional pressure was overwhelming. The political cost was career threatening. The rational move – the safe move – was to back down, go along, keep the peace the way his predecessor had.

Chris didn't fold. He held the line.

Not everyone abandoned him. Munib Malik, a newer hire from the law enforcement community, refrained from making a quick judgment. He and Chris had their moments of difficulty – transitions always do. But Munib watched. He observed the depth of what the LHPC framework offered agencies that really dug in. And once he saw it clearly, he stood squarely in defense of his leader.

That's what Political Capital looks like when it's built one relationship at a time, through demonstrated results rather than institutional position.

The moment the floor confirmed what the metrics hadn't yet.

While the resistance mounted above him, Chris looked down rather than up – and found two things that told him he wasn't wrong.

The first was attendance. Every week, Chris showed up to skill surge events we ran virtually for the LHPC teams – breathwork, discussions about the challenges they carried, moments of humor that let them see their directors and chiefs as human beings rather than a title. These weren't mandatory. Nobody required his people to be there. But they kept coming. Week after week, in a culture that had learned to expect nothing, his team chose to show up. That choice – small, quiet, easily overlooked – was evidence.

The second was a new hire who had become an unexpected influencer. She wasn't a supervisor. She had no formal authority. But something about the way Chris was building the culture had caught her attention, and she had started carrying it to the people around her. Newer staff were watching her watch him. The culture was beginning to travel laterally – peer to peer – before any survey had captured it.

Those two things didn't make the institutional battle easier. But they made it survivable. Sometimes making an impression on a small group is all it takes to sustain forward motion until the evidence catches up.

Meanwhile, something else was happening. The younger workforce – the people doing the work on the floor – started paying attention to who was fighting for them. They watched Chris take hits that would have broken someone less committed. They watched him keep showing up. They watched him refuse to abandon the vision even when his own leaders abandoned him.

They deemed him the influencer they wanted to follow.

2025 outcomes:

Depression indicators: Down from 31% to approximately 22%.

Compassion fatigue: Down from 59% to approximately 37%.

Survey response rate: Nearly doubled from 33% to 63%.

Staff using breathwork tools on the floor between crisis calls.

Fully staffed.

400+ applications every time they post a job opening.

That last number needs context. This is a 911 communications center in Canada – an industry hemorrhaging talent across the continent. Centers everywhere are understaffed, desperate, hiring anyone who applies. K Division is turning people away. They have the luxury of selection because their reputation now precedes them.

For the first time in memory, they are running without mandatory overtime. Dispatchers who had been working sixty-hour weeks for years suddenly have weekends again. People who haven't taken a vacation in two years are booking trips. But the deeper shift was operational: with full staffing, dispatchers can take time with complex calls instead of rushing to clear the queue. Quality is up. Errors are down. Training can happen without pulling someone off the floor.

The center started operating the way it was designed to operate – not in crisis mode, but in performance mode. One supervisor described it simply: "For the first time, we're not just surviving the shift. We're actually doing the job well." That's what fully staffed means. Not an absence of pain. The presence of capacity.

Other Operational Communications Centres throughout Canada are taking notice. They're watching what Chris and Jocelyn built – against everyone's bet – and asking how it happened. The agencies that dismissed LHPC as soft, unmeasurable, not serious work are now looking at staffing levels and application rates they can't explain away.

Chris still has detractors. The people who fought against him haven't disappeared. The institutional constraints of the RCMP haven't magically reformed. The union dynamics remain complicated.

But he won.

Not by making everyone happy. Not by avoiding conflict. Not by going along to get along. He won by being stubborn enough to outlast the resistance, by building evidence that made the results undeniable, by earning the loyalty of the people who do the work.

His staff describe a shift in mindset away from skepticism and toward something new:

"The belief that things can change and are getting better. That there are good things coming. People are more positive."

The goal Chris and Jocelyn share – a place where every member of their team knows they belong and is safe to fit where they're meant to be – isn't rhetoric. It's what they nearly lost their careers building.

That's what transformation costs. That's what grit produces. That's why the leaders who stay in this work are the leaders who change what everyone thought was possible.

The Dollar Translation

Fully staffed. Two words that hide the largest number in this story.

Industry-wide, 911 centers operate chronically understaffed. Every vacant position generates mandatory overtime that creates a burnout cascade – driving additional turnover, generating additional vacancies, generating additional overtime. It's a financial spiral that most centers treat as a fixed cost of doing business. K Division eliminated it. If the center was carrying even three vacancies prior to full staffing, the overtime savings alone represent $225,000 to $300,000 annually – recurring, compounding, and growing as the fully staffed center reduces burnout-driven departures going forward.

Four hundred applications per posting eliminated recruitment spend – advertising, job fairs, signing bonuses, background processing for candidates who wash out before they ever become operational. But the deeper savings come from selection power. When you choose from 400 instead of hiring from four, you select for training aptitude, cultural alignment, and longevity. Each percentage point reduction in washout rate saves a full training cycle. Over five years, better selection compounds into hundreds of thousands in avoided re-recruitment and retraining.

Depression dropping from 31% to 22% and compassion fatigue from 59% to 37% translates directly to reduced sick leave, lower healthcare claims, and fewer workers' comp filings for stress-related conditions. In law enforcement and emergency communications, stress-related claims average $15,000 to $45,000 per incident. A nine-point drop in depression prevalence represents multiple avoided claims annually.

Conservative annual financial impact: $500,000 or more. Built while its director was being told to stop.

Abilene Fire Department: The Embedded Influencer

Not every transformation comes from the top seat.

Michael Burden is the Deputy Fire Chief of Emergency Services for the Abilene Fire Department in Texas. He entered LHPC not as the positional head of an agency, but as a deputy — someone with significant responsibility but not total authority over his agency's direction.

He didn't let that stop him.

Chief Burden was hand-selected from more than one hundred applicants to join Leading High-Performance Cultures. That selection recognized something about him that even he didn't appreciate for the impressive characteristic it is: a leader who understood that culture isn't about position. It's about presence.

He found ways to embed culture change from wherever he stood. Quality one-on-one time with his bureau chiefs — not mandated meetings, but genuine investment in their development as leaders and as people. Physical discipline – he still works out every single day, maintaining the operational readiness of a firefighter half his age and rank. Living the standards of what I call the Peaceful Warrior Alpha.

> **PEACEFUL WARRIOR ALPHA** A leadership archetype characterized by the integration of empathy, engagement, discipline, and emotional calm. Strength without ego. Presence without domination. The ability to connect with a struggling employee at 2 PM and make a hard personnel decision at 3 PM without losing equilibrium in either moment. This is what mission-critical leadership looks like when it's fully developed – not the loudest person in the room, but the most grounded one.

Empathetic enough to connect, engaged enough to be present, disciplined enough to earn respect, and peaceful enough to lead without ego.

His influence spread beyond his formal authority.

I receive emails from Abilene Fire Department staff – people Chief Burden doesn't directly supervise – commenting on his impact within the agency. They watch him. They see who shows up consistently, who embodies the values instead of just posting them on a wall. More than 70% of his team reads my weekly newsletter. Not because it's required. Not because anyone mandated it. Because Chief Burden has created an appetite for growth that radiates outward from his example.

That number is not a culture metric. It's a prediction of retention.

Gallup's research on discretionary effort – doing more than what's required – shows that employees who consistently demonstrate it are 59% less likely to be actively seeking other employment. Seventy percent of a department voluntarily engaging with leadership development content on their own time is a workforce telling you, in behavior rather than words, that they've decided this organization is worth investing in. In a fire department where FEMA SAFER grants run approximately $90,000 per firefighter in years one and two, each person retained beyond the grant period represents avoided re-recruitment, retraining, and reapplication costs. Chief Burden's culture work is doing retention math that no benefits package can replicate – because the motivation is intrinsic, not compelled.

His bureau chiefs have responded to his leadership with visible engagement.

The moment presence became permission.

One of Chief Burden's bureau chiefs had never been the type to have personal conversations with his crew. He managed by task list – assignments, compliance, completion. After six months of Burden's one-on-one investment, something shifted.

The bureau chief started a practice nobody had explicitly taught him. He began each shift by walking through the station and making eye contact with every firefighter. Not saying anything directive. Not delivering instructions. Just being present. Acknowledging people.

Within weeks, the crew's dynamic changed. They started talking to each other differently. They started talking to him differently. And then, in a team meeting, a firefighter who hadn't spoken up in a year raised a safety concern.

That detail is easy to read past. Don't. Chief Burden didn't produce that outcome through a safety policy. He produced it by investing one-on-one in a bureau chief who changed how he showed up – and that bureau chief changed the dynamic of an entire crew by doing something that took thirty seconds and cost nothing. The firefighter who finally spoke up had been carrying that concern for months. What changed wasn't the concern. What changed was whether the room felt safe enough to say it out loud.

A firefighter who doesn't voice a concern about a compromised piece of equipment, a fatigue issue on a crew, or a structural read that doesn't feel right eventually becomes a workers' comp claim, a line-of-duty injury, or a NIOSH investigation. FEMA data consistently shows that departments with higher psychological safety have higher near-miss reporting rates – and higher reporting rates correlate directly with lower injury incidence. Each avoided line-of-duty injury represents $50,000 to $100,000 in workers' comp costs, plus overtime to cover the vacancy during recovery, plus the administrative burden of OSHA compliance.

Chief Burden didn't produce that outcome through a safety policy or a mandated reporting protocol. He produced it by investing one-on-one in a bureau chief who changed how he showed up for his crew. The bureau chief didn't learn presence from a training manual. He learned it from watching someone who believed presence was leadership. And a firefighter who had been silent for a year finally felt safe enough to speak.

That's the financial value of psychological safety: not what it produces when everything goes right, but what it prevents when something starts to go wrong.

Influence doesn't require authority. It requires consistency.

Within our LHPC cohort, Chief Burden became something unexpected: the linchpin.

The other directors and chiefs – people running entire agencies, facing their own institutional battles – look to him as an anchor. Not because he's the loudest or most accomplished. Because he brings support to other leaders at an intuitive level. He's profoundly humble yet strong enough that others want to follow him. In a cohort of high-performers fighting hard battles, he's the one who steadies the room.

Recently, the City of Abilene brought in a new city manager who has made culture a priority across all city departments. The external environment is catching up to what Chief Burden has been building quietly from the inside. The principles he's been living are now being validated by institutional attention he never sought.

Chief Burden doesn't have the metrics the other leaders in this chapter have. He doesn't control the budget, the hiring, or the agency-wide strategy. What he does have is something harder to measure and impossible to fake: the trust of people who've watched him long enough to know the difference between a leader who talks and a leader who is.

Intentional. Present. An alpha who doesn't need to look behind him to know his team follows right on his heels.

The Dollar Translation

Chief Burden's story requires a different financial lens – not because the dollars aren't there, but because they accumulate differently than in the other agencies in this chapter. There's no before-and-after eNPS swing, no turnover number that reversed, no staffing crisis that resolved. What there is, instead, is something harder to manufacture and more durable once built: a safety culture, a retention prediction, and a model of capital efficiency that no other story in this book can match.

Start with the safety concern. Near-miss reporting rates are one of the most financially significant cultural metrics in fire service, and they are almost entirely a function of psychological safety. A firefighter who feels unsafe speaking up doesn't file a near-miss report – they stay quiet, and the hazard persists. FEMA and NIOSH data consistently link departments with higher psychological safety to lower injury incidence. Each avoided line-of-duty injury represents $50,000 to $100,000 in workers' comp costs plus overtime coverage during recovery plus OSHA compliance burden. Chief

Burden didn't produce a safer crew through policy. He produced it by changing one bureau chief's behavior – and that bureau chief changed the dynamic of an entire crew. The firefighter who raised a concern after a year of silence represents the financial value of what didn't happen next.

Now scale to the 70% voluntary engagement figure. Gallup defines discretionary effort as doing more than the job requires – and employees who consistently demonstrate it are 59% less likely to be actively job-seeking. In a department where SAFER grants run $90,000 per firefighter in years one and two, each retained firefighter beyond the grant period avoids a full re-recruitment and retraining cycle. Chief Burden's voluntary engagement rate is a leading indicator that predicts those avoided costs before they show up in a retention number. The returns are real and they're growing.

But here's the argument that makes Abilene the most strategically significant story in this chapter:

The other leaders represented here spent real institutional resources to produce their results. Sheriff Miyamoto scheduled two hours per week per employee across a thousand-person department. Director James fought for institutional funding she eventually lost mid-transformation and built her results anyway. Director Spence nearly lost his career defending the investment his agency required him to make.

Chief Burden spent none of that. His investment was presence, consistency, and the attention he brought to one-on-one time with his bureau chiefs. The voluntary engagement, the raised safety concern, the crew dynamic that shifted – all of it came from a leader who changed behavior without authority, mandate, or budget line.

That ratio is the point.

Every agency represented in this chapter has a Michael Burden somewhere in its structure – a leader without the top seat who is either being developed or being overlooked. The agencies that find them, invest in them, and create conditions for their influence to scale are the ones that produce culture change at every level simultaneously, without waiting for the next director to arrive or the next budget cycle to open.

Chief Burden didn't need the top seat to change what was possible at Abilene. He needed someone to believe what he was already doing was worth developing.

That's the most capital-efficient investment in this book. And it's available to every leader reading it.

What the Evidence Reveals Together

Six agencies. Six different contexts. One framework. Viewed individually, each story makes its own case. Viewed together, patterns emerge that no single story can show.

The investment-to-return ratio is consistent across scale. San Francisco – 993 personnel – and Berrien County – a forty-person center – both show returns that dwarf their investment, despite operating at completely different scales. The framework doesn't require organizational size. It requires leadership commitment. The math works whether you're funding culture for a thousand people or forty.

The fastest financial returns come from stopping the bleed, not adding new programs. Every agency's biggest dollar recovery came from eliminating cultural waste that already existed – turnover they were already paying for, overtime they were already burning, recruitment costs they were already absorbing. The framework didn't create new expenses. It redirected money that was already being spent destructively toward investments that compound.

Institutional resistance doesn't prevent results. It delays them. The agencies with the most headwinds – Berrien County and K Division – show the clearest correlation between institutional constraints and unrealized financial potential. Berrien's energy vampire problem alone costs six figures annually. K Division built a fully staffed center while its director was being told to stop. Imagine what these agencies would produce if the systems they have no choice but to work within supported what they're building instead of constraining it.

Influence-based culture change is the most capital-efficient model. Chief Burden's story produces the lowest raw dollar total – but also the lowest investment cost. When culture change happens through voluntary engagement rather than mandated programs, the cost-per-outcome drops dramatically. Every agency would benefit from having a Michael Burden embedded at every level of its organization. The question is whether leaders above him create the conditions for that influence to scale. Imagine the impact he'd have if he were at the helm of an agency embracing high-performing culture change.

The compound effect is visible in agencies that started earliest. San Francisco – four years into the work – shows cumulative returns in the seven figures. F Division – eighteen months in – is generating six figures annually and accelerating. The agencies that started most recently show the steepest slopes of improvement but haven't yet reached the inflection point where compounding becomes dramatic. This is consistent with capital investment theory: early returns are linear, later returns are exponential.

The aggregate: $3.2 million in documented impact. That number is conservative. It counts what we can trace directly to culture metrics through recognized research methodologies – Gallup, SHRM, OSHA, CDC, McKinsey, WHO. It does not count the second-order effects: the institutional knowledge preserved when experienced employees stay, the safety incidents that didn't happen because peer trust was high, the recruitment costs that vanished because the reputation preceded the job posting, or the leadership development that multiplied through layers of the organization.

It does not count the career of the director who was nearly fired for building a healthy culture and now runs the most fully staffed center in his region. It does not count the fifteen-year employee who went from breaking to belonging because one leader believed in her. It does not count the deputy chief who changed an entire department's appetite for growth without ever holding the top seat.

The math makes the case. The stories reveal what the math can't capture.

What This Proves

Culture transformation isn't theoretical. It's measurable.

The agencies in this chapter aren't special. They don't have resources others lack. They don't have leadership that's inherently better. They have leaders who committed to a framework and worked it – against institutional resistance, through funding losses, around personnel they couldn't remove, past the point where most people would have quit. One of them doesn't even hold the top seat.

They have evidence that the investment pays off.

San Francisco: First net-positive retention in a decade.

F Division: World-class eNPS and zero turnover.

Bucks County: A skeptic transformed into an advocate, recruitment strategy revolutionized, dormant veterans reawakened.

Berrien County: Twelve-point eNPS swing against headwinds, with a peer-led culture initiative built from the floor.

K Division: A director who held the line when everyone told him to stop – now fully staffed with four hundred applicants per posting.

Abilene: A deputy chief embedding culture change without positional authority, his influence spreading so far that 70% of his team voluntarily engages with leadership content.

Six agencies. Six different contexts. One framework.

The evidence exists. The methodology works. The only variable is whether you'll commit to working it.

CHAPTER 4

THE PATH FORWARD

You've seen the framework. You've seen the evidence. The question is no longer whether culture transformation works. The question is whether you're ready to do what it requires.

A Direct Assessment

Before you decide anything, get honest about where you are.

Leadership Capital: Have you done your own work? Not attended a seminar – done the internal excavation that changes how you lead. Have you leaned into discomfort, or do you retreat to the familiar when growth gets uncomfortable? Do you know your why? Can you articulate it without reading it off a card? Does your team know what you stand for, or do they just know what you manage?

In a high-performing agency, staff can articulate their leader's brand. They reference it in peer conversations: "That's not how [Chief] would want us to handle this." The leader's values aren't just known – they've become the culture's operating system. If your team can't name what you stand for, that gap is costing you every day in decisions made without a compass.

The financial question: How many initiatives has your organization attempted in the past twenty-four months that stalled, failed, or required rework? For each one, add the direct investment plus the leadership time diverted to manage resistance. That total is your Leadership Trust price tag – and McKinsey's data says seventy percent of those failures trace back to employee resistance rooted in leadership distrust.

Human Capital: Are you scouting or just posting jobs and hoping? What happens to new hires in their first thirty days – do they feel like they belong, or like they're surviving initiation? What's your retention rate for employees under two years? If you don't know the number, that's your answer.

The financial question: How many people have you lost in the last twelve months? Multiply that number by your replacement cost per position – the figure you read in Chapter 3's anchor section. Then add the overtime your remaining staff worked to cover those vacancies. That total is what your current Human Capital gap is costing you annually. It's already in your budget. You're just not tracking it as culture.

Social Capital: What happens when someone makes a mistake? Do peers cover and coach, or do they distance and judge? Is information shared freely, or hoarded for advantage? When gossip starts, does anyone shut it down?

In a high-performing agency, when someone makes a mistake, the first response from peers is, "What happened and how do we fix it?" – not distance, not judgment, not documentation for leverage. Mistakes become learning moments because the culture has decided that protecting each other's growth matters more than protecting your own position. If your team's first instinct after a mistake is self-protection, that's your Social Capital score – regardless of what any survey says.

The financial question: Pull your workers' comp claims, safety incident reports, and sick leave patterns for the past twelve months. How many were driven or worsened by interpersonal conflict, communication failures, or stress from a toxic peer environment? Add the overtime generated by shift swap refusals and sick calls driven by interpersonal avoidance. That's your Social Capital price tag – and it's being paid whether you measure it or not.

Performance Capital: Are your standards written down? Are they enforced consistently – same standard for the veteran and the rookie, the favorite and the difficult? Does everyone on your team know what excellence looks like in their role, or do they just know what gets them in trouble?

The financial question: How many grievances, complaints, or internal investigations did inconsistent enforcement generate in the past year? Each one costs supervisor time, administrative processing, and in some cases legal exposure. How many disengaged employees are collecting full paychecks while delivering eighteen to thirty-four percent less productivity than their capable peers? That productivity gap, multiplied across your roster, is your Performance Capital deficit.

Professional Capital: Can your people see a future? Not a vague promise of advancement – a visible pathway with clear milestones. Are you developing people for their next role, or just extracting value from their current one? Are you promoting for merit or ease?

The financial question: How many departures in the last three years were people who left because they couldn't see a path forward? Each one represents the full cost of their training and development walking out the door, plus the replacement cost on the other side.

Financial Capital: Can you prove your culture investments work? Not in feelings – in numbers. Retention rates. Recruitment costs. Training ROI. If your budget is challenged tomorrow, could you defend it with evidence?

The financial question: Do you know what your culture is costing you right now – not in feelings, but in overtime, turnover, recruitment spending, workers' comp claims, and lost productivity? Can you walk into a budget meeting and present a specific dollar figure for what your organization is already spending on cultural waste? If you can't, every dollar you currently invest in culture is unprotected. And unprotected budget lines are the first ones cut.

Political Capital: Who has your back above you? If you got hit – loss of funding, personnel crisis, political attack – who would stand with you? If you left tomorrow, would the culture you're building survive your departure?

The financial question: What is the total investment your organization has made in culture over the past three to five years – leadership development, wellness programs, recruitment improvements, training systems? That's the number at risk in a leadership transition. If you don't have political capital protecting it, one new leader, one budget crisis, one shift in institutional priorities can zero out every dollar and every compounding return that investment was generating. Price the risk of losing it all. That's what Political Capital is worth.

Score yourself honestly. Not where you want to be. Where you are.

The leaders in this book started from hard places. They didn't start with advantages. They started with honesty about how far they had to go.

Now add up the financial questions. Every dollar you identified – the turnover costs, the overtime, the grievances, the lost productivity, the unprotected budget lines, the transition risk – is money your organization is already spending. It's just not being spent intentionally. That total is your cultural waste. And it's the number that should drive every decision you make from this point forward.

The Four Paths

From here, you have options.

Path 1: Self-Directed Implementation

Take what you've learned and apply it yourself.

You have the framework. You understand the sequence. You've seen what's possible. Some leaders will take this book, map it against their current reality, and start building.

This path works for leaders who have significant internal capacity, organizational support, and the discipline to hold themselves accountable over years without external structure. It's the lowest investment and the lowest probability of sustained transformation – not because the framework doesn't work, but because self-directed change rarely survives the daily pressures that caused the problems in the first place.

If you choose this path, commit to the sequence. Don't skip Leadership Capital because it feels self-indulgent. Don't jump to the interventions that seem most urgent before building the foundation that makes them work.

And don't close this book without momentum. Here are three things you can do this week that cost nothing:

One: Calculate your cultural waste. Use the financial questions above. Pull the numbers. Add them up. Write the total on a piece of paper and put it where you'll see it every day. That number is your case for everything that follows. Most leaders have never calculated it. The moment you do, you can't unsee it – and neither can anyone you show it to.

Two: Write your why statement – draft one. It won't be perfect. It doesn't need to be. Finish this sentence: "I [verb] [what you do] so that [the impact on others]." Director Spence's is "I believe in authenticity. I challenge perceptions so that reality replaces assumption." Yours will be different. The exercise matters more than the product. When you can name your driving motivation, you can start leading from it instead of from exhaustion.

Three: Have one conversation you've been avoiding. The team member who's struggling and you've been hoping it resolves itself. The standard that's slipping and you've been letting it slide. The supervisor who needs development and you haven't made time for it. Pick one. Have the conversation this week. Not a formal meeting. A real conversation – direct, respectful, and specific about what you need and why it matters. One conversation won't transform your culture. But it will break the pattern of avoidance that lets cultural waste accumulate.

Those three actions – calculate, articulate, engage – take less than two hours combined. They cost nothing. And they establish the foundation for every path that follows.

Path 2: Targeted Intervention

Address specific gaps with focused resources.

Maybe your leadership team needs Why Discovery. Maybe your recruitment process is broken, and Strategic Scouting would transform your applicant pool. Maybe you have the culture you want but no documentation to protect the budget that funds it.

Targeted intervention works for organizations that have genuine strengths but specific weaknesses. It's higher investment than self-direction but more focused than full transformation. The risk is treating symptoms without addressing root causes – fixing recruitment while ignoring the leadership patterns that drive people away after you hire them.

If you choose this path, be honest about whether the gap you're targeting is actually the gap that matters most. The presenting problem is rarely the real problem.

Path 3: Comprehensive Transformation

Multi-year, supported implementation of the full framework.

This path is for leaders who have done the honest assessment in the previous section and concluded that the gaps are too deep for self-direction to close, the obstacles too entrenched for targeted intervention to address, and the stakes too high to accept the probability that both will fail.

It's also for leaders who know themselves well enough to recognize that accountability structures aren't a luxury. They're the difference between good intentions that survive the first quarter and a commitment that holds through year four when the culture has improved enough that the urgency fades, but not enough that the work is done. The leaders in this book didn't complete the work because conditions were favorable. They completed it because they had a framework, a cohort of peers fighting the same battles, and someone who had watched enough leaders make the same costly mistakes to tell them when they were about to make one.

We select for fit, not size or resources. A forty-person dispatch center and a thousand-person sheriff's department have both worked this path, and the framework scales to both. What it doesn't scale to is leaders who aren't ready – and readiness isn't a credential. It's a decision. The leaders who dropped out of the cohorts represented in this book weren't less experienced than the ones who stayed. They were less willing to stay uncomfortable long enough for the discomfort to produce something.

Seven years into comprehensive transformation, the agency operates differently at every level. New hires don't just survive their first year. They thrive in it, because every person they encounter reinforces the same culture from day one. Veterans aren't counting down to retirement. They're mentoring the next generation because someone gave their experience a purpose beyond endurance. And when a difficult call comes in, the team responds with precision, supports each other through the aftermath, and walks out knowing they belong somewhere that will never ask them to carry it alone.

For leaders whose engagement has ignited rather than satisfied their appetite for this work, the journey doesn't end at Phase 5. The Act 2 / LHPC Master Certification pathway opens at graduation – a Certified LHPC Master designation, co-authoring opportunities, and co-presenting at national conferences alongside Pathfinder Resilience. This is the pathway for the leader who has transformed their agency and now wants to transform the profession. Not an ending. A launch point.

That's not a promise. That's what the evidence in Chapter 3 documents.

Path 4: Do Nothing

Continue current trajectory.

I include this because it's the path most people choose. Not consciously – they simply never make a different choice. They read books, attend conferences, nod along with frameworks, and return to organizations that absorb them back into the same patterns.

If you choose this path, choose it consciously.

The problems you have today will be bigger tomorrow. The culture you're not building intentionally is being built anyway – by whoever's loudest, whoever's most persistent, whoever fills the vacuum you've left.

Three years of doing nothing doesn't look like standing still. It looks like the best employee on your team – the one everyone relies on during mass casualty events – handing in his resignation because he got tired of watching the organization tolerate what he couldn't. Doing nothing doesn't cost you money in the abstract. It costs you specific people – the ones you can least afford to lose – because the 1% of the 4% won't stay in an environment that asks them to shrink.

Doing nothing is a choice. Just make sure you understand what you're choosing.

The financial reality: Add up the cultural waste you identified in the assessment above. That number doesn't shrink with time – it compounds. Each departure drives more overtime, which drives more burnout, which drives more departures. Each year without investment is a year the spiral accelerates. Inaction has a price. It's just not on a line item – which is exactly why it never gets addressed.

What If You're Not the Top Leader?

Every example in this book has been a director, sheriff, or chief – someone in the top seat with authority to mandate, allocate, and decide.

But what if that's not you?

Michael Burden answered that question. The principle is simple: you don't need the top seat to transform culture. You need the commitment to live it so consistently that others can't help but notice the contrast.

Start where you are. Live what you believe. Let the influence compound.

The First 90 Days

Most leaders who reach this point in the book have made a decision. They just haven't felt it yet.

This is what feeling it looks like.

It begins before any metric is collected or any framework is introduced into the culture. It starts with a single conversation – the Resilience Why Discovery – that happens away from the office, away from the inbox, away from the operational noise that has been filling every available hour for years.

The conversation starts with a question most leaders have never been asked: *Tell me about your earliest memory.*

And then it keeps going.

For three hours or more, a leader tells the story of their life. Not the professional biography – the real one. The events that shaped them. The losses they absorbed. The moments they didn't know how to name until someone asked the right question and the answer arrived before they could stop it. Things said out loud for the first time. Things they hadn't considered about themselves until a different kind of listening made space for them to surface.

This is the Resilience Why Discovery. Not an assessment. Not a personality inventory. A human conversation about how a person was forged – and what that forging reveals about why they lead the way they do.

A few weeks pass. Notes become a theme breakdown. The leader returns for a second meeting.

And this time, they hear themselves reflected back.

Not evaluated. Not coached toward a predetermined outcome. Seen. In the specific way that only happens when someone has listened carefully enough to name what you've been carrying without knowing it had a name. Leaders who have spent careers projecting certainty sit with that reflection and go quiet in the same way they went quiet when their agency's why statement landed in Chapter 2's description of the framework.

Because this is where that statement comes from. Not from a workshop exercise. From the excavation of the life that built them for exactly this work.

That is the first moment the magic takes root.

What follows is a sequence, not an event. The baseline assessment captures the financial picture of where the agency stands before any work begins – giving the leader a number that finally names what they've been sensing for years. The cohort connects. The work begins.

The walls come down faster when you already know who you are.

Six weeks in, something small changes. Not a metric. A behavior. A Monday briefing that opens differently than it ever has. A conversation with a supervisor that goes somewhere it never went before. A staff member who stops by to say something that wouldn't have been said three months ago. The leader notices it before anyone else does. And in that noticing – in that small, private recognition that something is different – the work stops being a framework and becomes theirs.

That's what the first 90 days produce. Not transformation. The beginning of belief that transformation is possible.

Everything in Chapter 3 started there.

The Commitment Required

Whatever path you choose, be clear about what real transformation demands.

Time. Five to seven years. Not seven months.

This is the number that scares people off. They want results now. They want to show progress before the next budget cycle, the next election, the next leadership transition.

Cultural transformation doesn't work on that timeline. You can show early indicators – engagement shifts, retention improvements, climate survey movement. But the deep change, the kind that survives leadership transitions and budget crises and the inevitable resistance? That takes years.

The five-phase structure exists because transformation follows a construction sequence. Each phase builds what the next one requires. Phase 1 lays the foundation. Phase 5 ensures the building stands after you're no longer in the room. Anyone promising faster is selling you a program. You're building something designed to last.

Energy. Consistent leadership attention.

Not just budget approval – presence. Not just delegation to HR – involvement. The directors in this book didn't hand this off. They showed up. They communicated. They modeled what they were asking others to become.

Resources. Real budget allocation.

Not leftovers. Not "whatever's available after operations." Strategic investment with protected funding.

Culture work gets cut first when budgets tighten – unless you've built the evidence case that makes cutting it obviously foolish. The agencies that survive budget battles are the ones that can prove ROI in language CFOs understand. Build that case from day one.

Courage. Willingness to embrace discomfort.

Assessment reveals reality. Sometimes reality is uncomfortable. The data might show that your leadership team isn't trusted. That your standards aren't enforced consistently. That the person you promoted is part of the problem. That your own patterns are creating dysfunction.

But courage isn't just about hearing hard truths. It's about leaning into experiences that feel foreign – approaches that challenge everything you think you know. The leaders who transform are the ones who hear hard truths and act on them instead of explaining them away.

Tenacity. Commitment that outlasts resistance.

It will get hard. The people who benefit from the current culture will push back. The quick wins will fade and the long slog will begin. There will be a moment – probably several – when quitting seems reasonable.

The leaders in this book hit those moments. They didn't quit. They showed up for each other. That's why they have results worth documenting.

The Challenge

Your team needs you to be brave.

They need you to discover your why and live it – not as a slogan on your wall, but as a compass that guides decisions when decisions are hard.

They need you to show up consistently. Not with polished messaging – with real presence. In their space. Visible. Accessible. Human.

They need you to set a high bar. Not because you enjoy demanding things, but because they want to know what they're capable of. High performers don't want easy. They want meaningful challenges with someone who believes they can meet them.

They need you to see them. Not as headcount or FTEs or interchangeable resources — as individuals with different motivations, different needs, different potential. The Gen X veteran who's been coasting needs something different than the Gen Z new hire who's questioning everything. Both need to be seen.

They need you to fight for them. Against institutional policies that don't fit mission-critical reality. Against budget cuts that would gut what you're building. Against the toxic personnel who poison the culture while policies created for the 96% demand more documentation.

They need you to build something worth staying for. Because right now, many of them are wondering whether this organization is where they want to build their career — or just where they're marking time until something better appears.

The Culture Capital Series

This book is the gateway. It establishes the framework and makes the case.

But the detailed playbooks — the specific how for each type of capital — come in the books that follow:

Leadership Capital: The Foundation of High-Performing Cultures — Deep dive on developing leaders who drive transformation. Why discovery, strategic mapping, personal brand, multi-generational influence.

Human Capital: Investing in People for High-Performing Cultures – The complete talent lifecycle. Strategic scouting, Recruiting for the 4%, DNA onboarding, wellbeing systems, retention architecture.

Social Capital: Creating Trust in High-Performing Cultures – Trust networks, peer support, collaborative systems. The invisible connective tissue.

Performance Capital: Building Systems for High-Performing Cultures – Standards, accountability, measurement. The operational backbone that turns values into behaviors.

Professional Capital: Developing Expertise in High-Performing Cultures – Career pathway mapping, reputation building, knowledge transfer. How careers become legacies.

Financial Capital: Strategic Resourcing for High-Performing Cultures – Budget protection, ROI documentation, economic sustainability. Making it last.

Political Capital: Building Influence for High-Performing Cultures – Stakeholder management, succession planning, strategic positioning. Surviving transitions.

Each book gives you the detailed playbook for one capital type. Together, they're the complete guide to the 7C+ Framework.

The Decision

I told you at the beginning that this book is for the 1% of the 4%.

Four percent of the population is hardwired for mission-critical work.

One percent of those four percent pursue excellence at the level of cultural leadership. They're not satisfied with surviving their environment –

they want to transform it. They see what their organization could become and they're willing to fight to build it.

You're still reading. That suggests you might be one of them.

The methodology exists. The framework is clear. The evidence is documented across six agencies with $3.2 million in measurable impact.

The question isn't whether you're capable. The leaders in Chapter 3 prove you are.

The question is whether you're ready.

Conclusion: The Leaders We Scout

Rodger and I have been doing this work long enough to recognize what we're looking for. When a leader walks into our process, we're not evaluating their credentials or their track record or their agency's size. We're looking for something harder to measure.

We're looking at who God made them to be.

Unique. Purposeful. Passionate. Fully capable.

We see it before they do. We saw it in Jocelyn before she stopped micromanaging. We saw it in Chris before he proved he could outlast the resistance. We saw it in John before he learned to embrace discomfort. We saw it in Michael before he became the linchpin his peers would come to depend on.

They didn't need to become different people. They needed to realize their own unique skills and the potential that comes from honing them. They needed someone they respect to believe in them and invest in them. They needed someone to reflect back what they couldn't see in themselves.

That's the differentiator.

We meet all kinds of leaders. Some are so self-focused they believe themselves to be the answer to every problem – and those leaders can't be helped because they're not actually looking for it. They're looking for validation of what they've already decided. Others are so convinced of their own inadequacy that they can't get past someone wanting to invest in them – and those leaders struggle to receive what we're offering because receiving feels like admitting need.

But there's a third kind of leader. The ones we're looking for.

They're humble enough to know they don't have all the answers – but passionate enough to keep searching. They're hopeful, even when the evidence doesn't support hope yet. They're optimistic without being naive. They still carry an attitude of awe and wonder about what this work could become.

These are the leaders who can take what we teach and tailor it to their leadership style and agency parameters without being arrogant about refusing to use 100% of the tools. They understand that agency policy and procedures can be met while subtly influencing at a different pace or angle – without wholeheartedly tossing the entire toolkit out the window because one piece doesn't fit their context.

They don't love adversity. No one actually loves adversity. But they won't avoid it if it means coming out on the other side stronger. They've learned – or they're learning – that the discomfort of growth is better than the discomfort of regret.

The resilient ones.

The teachable ones.

The ones who still believe something extraordinary is possible.

Here's what I know after fifteen years in this work.

The leaders who transform cultures aren't the ones who arrive certain. They're the ones who arrive uncertain – and do the work anyway.

The leaders who build high-performing teams aren't the ones without wounds. They're the ones who face their wounds, name them, and refuse to let those wounds run their leadership.

The leaders who create lasting change aren't the ones who have all the answers. They're the ones who stay humble enough to keep asking questions, stay teachable enough to apply what they learn, and stay brave enough to try things that might not work.

That's the only requirement. Not certainty. Willingness.

Picture this: It's 6:47 AM. A dispatcher walks into her center for the start of shift. She passes a wall where her team's why statements are displayed – not as corporate art, but as evidence of conversations that changed how they see each other. She sits at her console next to a colleague who asks about her daughter's soccer game. She takes her first call – a father reporting his child missing – and her voice is steady, her protocols are automatic, her focus is total. When the call ends, she takes one breath, uses the technique she learned six months ago, and takes the next call.

During a break, her supervisor stops by. Not to check her numbers. To say, "That missing child call was textbook. Well done."

She finishes her shift. She drives home. She doesn't carry the weight alone because she works in a place that taught her she doesn't have to. She'll be back tomorrow. Not because she has to be. Because she wants to be.

That's a high-performing culture. Not a poster. Not a program. A place where people built for extraordinary work get to do extraordinary work – and the organization is built to invest in them while they do it.

Culture is remembered, not invented. Your high-performing culture is waiting to be built.

We believe that when we invest in leaders who want to change the world, they will.

Are you among them?

What Happens Next Is Up to You

You've just seen the roadmap. The question is whether you're the kind of leader who puts it on a shelf – or one who puts it to work.

The Leading High-Performing Cultures Mastermind was built for the rare leader who refuses to accept mediocrity as an operational standard. It's not for everyone. It's for the ones who recognize that culture is the mission – and are ready to build something that proves it.

If that's you, the next step is an application, not a registration. Because the leaders in this room are selected, not simply enrolled.

Learn more at <u>pathfinderresilience.com</u>.

THE LANGUAGE OF A HIGH-PERFORMING CULTURE

Terms Worth Knowing

Every profession has language that insiders take for granted and outsiders never learned. Mission-critical work is no different. We talk about culture, trust, resilience, and wellness as though everyone shares the same definitions. They don't.

What follows are the terms you've encountered throughout this book. Some are familiar words used in unfamiliar ways. Some are concepts you've experienced but never had language for. Some are measurements your CFO needs to understand if you're ever going to get budget approval for the work this book describes.

These aren't academic definitions. They're behavioral ones. Each term is defined by what it looks like in practice – in your hallways, on your floor, in the conversations your people are having when you're not in the room.

This section is not a glossary to skim. It's the foundation the rest of the book is built on. Read it now. Return to it later. Everything that follows assumes you understand it.

WHO WE'RE TALKING ABOUT

Every culture has them. Two types of people whose impact on those around them compounds in opposite directions. One eroding. One accelerating. Understanding the difference between them is the beginning of understanding why culture transformation is both urgent and possible.

Energy Vampire – A team member whose persistent negativity, resistance, or toxicity actively erodes the cultural health of those around them. This isn't a personality conflict. It's a person who creates a ceiling on how far your culture can rise. Staff know exactly who they are. Leadership usually does too. The question is whether anyone has the institutional support to act.

The inverse is equally real. A **cultural catalyst** is the team member who, when a new hire makes a mistake on a live call, walks over during the next break and says, "Your instincts were right. Here's the one piece you were missing." That interaction takes forty-five seconds. It converts a potential confidence collapse into acceleration. Energy vampires erode. Cultural catalysts compound.

The 4% – Approximately four percent of the population is psychologically hardwired for mission-critical work. They possess ten specific psychological skills – including elevated sensation-seeking, hardiness under stress, internal locus of control, and discomfort with equilibrium – that can't be taught. These skills are default wiring, not learned behaviors. Your dispatchers, firefighters, officers, and paramedics who thrive under pressure aren't just trained well. They're built differently. The remaining 96% can do many jobs competently. They cannot sustain the psychological demands of yours.

The 1% of the 4% – Within that four percent, a smaller subset pursues excellence at the level of cultural leadership. They're not satisfied with surviving their environment. They want to transform it. They see what their organization could become and they're willing to fight to build it. These are the leaders this book is written for.

Mission-Critical Professionals – Personnel whose work involves life-and-death stakes, relentless stress, and zero margin for error. The environments where a bad shift doesn't mean a missed deadline. It means someone doesn't go home.

THE FRAMEWORK

The 7C+ Framework – The architecture for cultural transformation introduced in this book. Seven distinct types of capital investment – Leadership, Human, Performance, Professional, Social, Financial, and Political – deployed in three strategic phases, amplified by two force multipliers (Fun and Artifacts), and calibrated through a multi-generational lens. The "+" represents the multipliers that accelerate every investment.

Capital Investment vs. Program – A capital investment allocates resources to build assets that appreciate over time and generate ongoing returns. A leader developed today develops other leaders for years. A program is a one-time expenditure that depreciates immediately. Motivational speakers come, leave, and the uplifting feeling evaporates. This book argues that culture has been treated as a program when it should be treated as capital. Programs create moments. Capital investments create assets. The distinction is the difference between inspiration that fades by Wednesday and a leadership shift that compounds for years.

The Three Phases – Foundation (Years 1 – 2), Expansion (Years 2 – 4), and Sustainability (Years 4 – 8). Culture transformation follows a construction sequence. Building in the wrong order wastes resources and erodes credibility. The phases define what gets built when – and why skipping ahead collapses what you're trying to construct.

DNA Onboarding – A culture-immersion process designed to transfer organizational identity to new hires from day one. Traditional orientation covers policies, paperwork, and building tours. DNA Onboarding communicates who we are, why we exist, and what it means to belong here. The goal is that a new hire feels the culture before they've learned the systems.

Strategic Scouting – The intentional identification and pursuit of candidates who possess the psychological profile for mission-critical work. This replaces traditional recruitment, which posts openings and screens whoever applies. Scouting means you know what you're looking for before a position is vacant, and you're building relationships with potential candidates long before they see a job listing.

Why Discovery – The structured process of identifying and articulating your core driving motivation – the reason you do what you do that persists regardless of role, rank, or organization. A personal why statement isn't a slogan. It's a compass. When a leader makes her purpose visible, it changes how she leads.

Pattern Interrupt – Any deliberate disruption of habitual thinking or behavior designed to create space for new patterns to form. Growth requires unfamiliar territory. The annual Mastermind experience on Mackinac Island in Michigan was created as a pattern interruption for our invited leaders.

Cultural Artifacts – The physical and tangible elements that reinforce a high-performing mindset. Why statements displayed throughout facilities. Visual elements in operational spaces that signal values. Environmental design that supports the behaviors you're building. These aren't decorations. They're reminders that create accountability. When your values are on the wall, people notice when behavior contradicts them.

WHAT WE MEASURE

The Current State Assessment captures seven culture markers. Each measures a specific dimension of organizational health. Each has a dollar value attached to it – because every deficit in these areas is costing your agency money right now, whether you've calculated it or not.

Chapter 2 explores each marker in depth. Chapter 3 shows you what they look like in real agencies. The Appendix gives you the formulas to calculate your own numbers. Here's what you need to know now:

Peer Trust – The quality of horizontal relationships across your workforce. When it's high, conflicts resolve faster, knowledge transfers naturally, and new hires integrate quickly. When it's low, every interaction carries friction. The dollar cost shows up in operational errors, safety incidents, and the overtime required to manage interpersonal dysfunction.

Supervisor Trust – The quality of the relationship between frontline personnel and their direct supervisors. This is the single strongest predictor of voluntary turnover. People don't leave organizations. They leave supervisors.

Leadership Trust – The quality of the relationship between the workforce and executive leadership. Distinct from supervisor trust. An employee can trust their sergeant and distrust the chief. When leadership trust is low, every initiative encounters resistance. Policies get complied with on paper and undermined in practice.

Workplace Wellbeing – The environmental quality of the work experience. This measures the organization, not the individual. Purpose, belonging, psychological safety, culture fit. Workplace wellbeing is the buffer that protects mission-critical personnel from the cumulative toll of trauma, danger, and stress. When that buffer fails, absenteeism rises, healthcare costs escalate, and operational readiness deteriorates.

eNPS (Employee Net Promoter Score) – A single-question measurement of workforce loyalty: "How likely are you to recommend this organization as a place to work?" Scored on a 0 – 10 scale. Promoters (9 – 10) minus Detractors (0 – 6) gives you a score from -100 to +100. Above 0 means more advocates than critics. Above 50 is excellent. The dollar value runs directly through recruitment costs. When your score is negative, your own people are making it harder to hire.

Individual Wellness – The personal health status of each team member. Physical and mental health, stress levels, coping capacity, feelings of overwhelm, career entrapment. Unlike workplace wellbeing, which measures the environment, individual wellness assesses the person. The dollar cost shows up as presenteeism – the invisible productivity drain when people are physically present but mentally depleted.

Culture Fit – The alignment between the individual and the organization. Retention intent, sense of belonging, and whether the person's wiring matches what the mission and culture demand. This is your early warning system. Research shows that roughly fifty percent of employees expressing intent to leave actually depart within twelve months.

Together, these seven markers make culture auditable. When you can measure each one and trace it to a financial outcome, you have something you can take to a budget meeting. You have something a CFO can evaluate. You have something a board can protect.

THE FINANCIAL LANGUAGE

Culture has always had a cost. The problem is that most organizations have never calculated it. These terms give you the vocabulary to translate culture into the language your CFO, city manager, or board already speaks.

Cost per Vacancy – The total financial impact of an unfilled position, including recruitment, training, overtime coverage, reduced capacity during the learning curve, and administrative burden. In mission-critical fields, this ranges from $50,000 to $150,000 per vacancy depending on role and training pipeline length. This is the number you'll see referenced throughout the book. It's the single most important figure in your cultural waste calculation.

Presenteeism – The hidden productivity loss when employees are physically present but mentally disengaged. A dispatcher at the console but checked out. A supervisor who stopped caring three years ago but shows up every shift. *Research estimates presenteeism costs organizations two to three times more than absenteeism*, because it affects quality, safety, and decision-making without triggering any alarm.

Trust Tax – The measurable cost imposed on every transaction, communication, and decision in a low-trust environment. High-trust organizations move faster. Low-trust organizations document everything, require approval chains for routine decisions, and meet resistance at every turn. That drag on speed and efficiency has a dollar value.

Trust Dividend – The inverse of the trust tax. The measurable acceleration in speed, efficiency, and performance that high-trust environments produce. Every investment in trust compounds: decisions move faster, conflicts resolve cheaper, talent stays longer, and reputation does the recruiting.

Cultural Waste – Money your organization is already spending that produces no return because of cultural dysfunction. The overtime driven by vacancies caused by turnover caused by broken supervisor trust. The recruitment costs inflated by a negative eNPS. The training investment lost when a new hire leaves in year one. You are already paying for culture. The question is whether you're paying for the culture you want – or paying the consequences of the one you have.

Compound Returns – The accelerating effect of capital investment over time. A leader developed today develops other leaders who develop others. Trust built this year reduces friction for years. Unlike programs, which depreciate immediately, capital investments appreciate. Your CFO understands compounding. Use that language.

THE PSYCHOLOGICAL LANGUAGE

Psychological Safety – The shared belief that the team environment is safe for interpersonal risk-taking. Speaking up about a concern. Admitting a mistake. Raising a challenge to someone with more rank. Psychological safety doesn't mean avoiding hard conversations. It means people trust that hard conversations won't be weaponized against them.

Compassion Fatigue – The gradual erosion of empathy, hope, and emotional capacity that results from prolonged exposure to others' suffering. Distinct from burnout, which results from organizational dysfunction.

Compassion fatigue doesn't mean they've stopped caring. It means their capacity to care has been depleted without being replenished.

Understimulation (The Misdiagnosis) – The condition where mission-critical professionals are incorrectly diagnosed as burned out when they're actually suffering from insufficient challenge, meaning, or autonomy. The 4% are psychologically wired to seek intensity. When the work becomes routine, when leadership stops developing them, when the culture asks them to shrink instead of grow, they don't burn out. They shut down. It looks like burnout. It feels like burnout. But the treatment is opposite: not rest and recovery, but meaningful challenge and investment. This misdiagnosis costs agencies their best people, because they prescribe wellness days for someone who needs a mission worth fighting for.

Locus of Control – The degree to which a person believes outcomes are determined by their own actions versus external forces. Mission-critical professionals with an internal locus of control believe they can influence results through their decisions, effort, and skill. This is one of the ten psychological skills that define the 4%. It's also why top-down mandates without input create resistance. People wired to control outcomes don't respond well to being told their input doesn't matter.

Peaceful Warrior Alpha – A leadership archetype characterized by the integration of empathy, engagement, discipline, and emotional calm. Strength without ego. Presence without domination. The ability to connect with a struggling employee at 2 PM and make a hard personnel decision at 3 PM without losing equilibrium in either moment. This is what mission-critical leadership looks like when it's fully developed.

Rational (Keirsey Temperament) – One of four temperament types in the Keirsey framework, characterized by strategic thinking, systems orientation, and skepticism toward anything that can't be measured. Rationals live in logic and data. They're naturally resistant to approaches that feel intuitive or emotional. Several leaders in this book are Rationals, and their transformation required embracing the discomfort of modalities that didn't fit their wiring.

One final term.

Culture Equation – The premise of this book. Culture is not accidental, aspirational, or abstract. It is the sum of specific, measurable investments made in a specific sequence over a specific period. Like any equation, change the inputs and you change the output. Neglect a variable and the equation breaks. The Culture Equation is the formula for building organizations worth staying for – expressed in the same discipline, the same rigor, and the same financial accountability you'd apply to any capital project. Because that's exactly what it is.

APPENDIX

CULTURE CAPITAL WORKSHEET

Your numbers. Your agency. Your case for investment.

This worksheet contains every formula referenced in Chapters 2 through 4. No explanatory prose. No stories. Just the math your CFO needs to see. Fill in your agency's numbers, calculate your cultural waste, and bring the totals to your next budget meeting.

Photocopy this section. Write in the margins. Dog-ear the pages. This is a working tool, not a display piece.

SECTION 1: YOUR AGENCY PROFILE

Field	Your Number
Agency name	
Total authorized positions	
Current filled positions	
Current vacancies	
Annual operating budget	
Annual personnel budget (salaries + benefits)	
Average annual salary (fully loaded)	
Average overtime rate (hourly)	
Departures in last 12 months	
Average time-to-fill (days)	
Training pipeline length (weeks)	
First-year washout rate (%)	

SECTION 2: CULTURE MARKERS SCORECARD

Record your Current State Assessment scores. Benchmark ranges from LHPC agency data.

Marker	Your Score	Crisis	Healthy	World-Class
Peer Trust		Below 50%	70 – 85%	Above 85%
Supervisor Trust		Below 50%	70 – 85%	Above 90%
Leadership Trust		Below 40%	60 – 80%	Above 80%
Workplace Wellbeing		Below 50%	65 – 80%	Above 85%
eNPS		Below 0	+10 to +30	Above +50
Individual Wellness		Below 50%	65 – 80%	Above 85%
Culture Fit		Below 50%	70 – 85%	Above 90%

Scores in the Crisis column indicate active financial bleed. See Section 3 to calculate the dollar cost.

SECTION 3: FINANCIAL FORMULAS

Each formula corresponds to a capital investment from the 7C+ Framework. Calculate each line, then carry totals to Section 4.

Leadership Capital

Supervisor-driven turnover cost

Departures attributed to supervisor issues x Replacement cost per position

= $ __________

Source: Gallup (75% of voluntary turnover traces to direct supervisor)

Decision bottleneck cost

Hours per week leadership spends on decisions staff could make x Leader hourly rate x 52 = $ _________

Source: McKinsey (decision-making speed correlates with organizational performance)

Human Capital

Total replacement cost

Departures in last 12 months x Replacement cost per position = $

____

Source: SHRM (replacement cost = 50 – 200% of annual salary depending on role)

Vacancy overtime cost

Current vacancies x Overtime hours per vacancy per week x OT rate x 52

= $ _________

Source: Industry standard (each vacancy generates 10 – 20 hours weekly mandatory OT)

Washout cost

Hires in last 12 months x Washout rate x Training investment per hire = $ _________

Source: SHRM (first-year turnover represents total training loss)

Performance Capital

Presenteeism cost

Employees reporting low wellness x Average salary x 0.18 to 0.34 = $ _________

Source: Gallup (disengaged employees operate at 18 – 34% reduced productivity)

Absenteeism cost

Unscheduled absence days per year (agency-wide) x Daily backfill cost = $ _________

Source: CDC Workforce Health (absenteeism costs $3,600 per hourly employee annually)

Professional Capital

Training investment at risk

Employees expressing intent to leave x Training cost per employee = $ _________

Source: Research indicates ~50% of those expressing intent to leave depart within 12 months

Development gap cost

Supervisors without formal leadership training x Estimated cost of poor decisions per supervisor per year = $ _________

Source: McKinsey (untrained managers make costlier decisions across hiring, conflict resolution, scheduling)

Social Capital

Conflict resolution cost

Hours per week spent managing interpersonal conflict x Supervisor hourly rate x 52 = $ _________

Source: CPP Global (U.S. employees spend 2.8 hours per week in conflict)

Toxic employee cost

Number of identified toxic employees x 2 driven departures per year x Replacement cost = $ _________

Source: Harvard Business School (toxic workers drive out an average of 2 good employees annually)

Financial Capital

eNPS recruitment impact

eNPS score x Number of employees x $940 = $ _________ (positive = savings, negative = cost)

Source: Bain/Temkin Group (each eNPS point correlates with ~$940 per employee in financial growth)

Recruitment spend (current)

Cost per hire (advertising + processing + background + onboarding) x Hires per year = $ _________

Source: SHRM (average cost-per-hire in public safety exceeds national averages due to background requirements)

Political Capital

Institutional resistance cost

Initiatives stalled or blocked by lack of stakeholder support x Estimated cost per stalled initiative = $ _________

Source: Organizational change research (lack of stakeholder buy-in is the #1 reason initiatives fail)

Stress-related claims cost

Workers' comp filings for stress-related conditions in last 12 months x Average claim cost ($15,000 – $45,000) = $ _________

Source: OSHA/CDC (stress-related claims in public safety average $15K – $45K per incident)

SECTION 4: CULTURAL WASTE CALCULATOR

Carry your totals from Section 3. This is the number you bring to the budget meeting.

Category	Annual Cost
Leadership Capital waste	
Human Capital waste	
Performance Capital waste	
Professional Capital waste	
Social Capital waste	
Financial Capital waste	
Political Capital waste	
TOTAL ANNUAL CULTURAL WASTE	$ ____________

This number represents money your agency is already spending. Culture investment does not add a new budget line. It redirects money currently being spent on dysfunction toward investments that compound.

SECTION 5: REPLACEMENT COST QUICK REFERENCE

Use the range that fits your agency's role and training pipeline. This is the anchor number for most calculations above.

Role Type	Replacement Range	Your Estimate
911 Dispatcher / Telecommunicator	$50,000 – $75,000	
Law Enforcement Officer	$75,000 – $150,000	
Firefighter / Paramedic	$75,000 – $120,000	
Corrections Officer	$50,000 – $100,000	
Supervisor / Sergeant	$100,000 – $150,000	
Mid-level Manager / Lieutenant	$100,000 – $175,000	

Includes: separation processing, recruitment advertising, background investigation, academy/training, field training, reduced productivity during learning curve, overtime coverage during vacancy, and administrative burden. Sources: SHRM, OSHA, industry benchmarks.

SECTION 6: ROI PROJECTION

Estimate returns based on LHPC agency outcomes documented in Chapter 3.

Metric	Your Projection
Total cultural waste (from Section 4)	
Conservative recovery target: 25% of waste in Year 1	
Moderate recovery target: 40% of waste in Year 2	
Full compound target: 60 – 75% of waste by Year 4	
Annual investment in culture (LHPC or equivalent)	
PROJECTED YEAR 1 ROI	_____________ : 1

LHPC agencies documented in this book range from 3:1 to 12:1 ROI depending on agency size, starting conditions, and institutional support. The agencies that started earliest show the highest cumulative returns, consistent with compound investment theory.

SECTION 7: RESEARCH SOURCES

Every formula in this worksheet is grounded in recognized research. Listed here for citation in budget proposals.

Source	What It Establishes
Gallup	Disengagement costs 18 – 34% productivity. 75% of voluntary turnover traces to supervisor. Engaged teams show 23% higher profitability.
SHRM	Replacement cost = 50 – 200% of annual salary. Average cost-per-hire benchmarks. Turnover rate benchmarks by industry.
CDC	Absenteeism costs $3,600 per hourly employee annually. Workplace stress contributes to healthcare cost escalation.
OSHA	Stress-related workers' comp claims average $15K – $45K per incident in public safety.
McKinsey	Decision-making speed correlates with top-quartile organizational performance. Untrained managers compound costs across operations.
WHO	Depression and anxiety cost the global economy $1 trillion annually in lost productivity. ROI on workplace mental health investment: $4 for every $1 spent.

Source	What It Establishes
Bain / Temkin	Each eNPS point correlates with approximately $940 per employee in financial growth.
Harvard Business School	A single toxic employee drives out an average of 2 good employees per year. Toxic worker cost exceeds the value added by a top performer.
CPP Global	U.S. employees spend an average of 2.8 hours per week dealing with conflict. Estimated annual cost: $359 billion in paid hours.
FEMA SAFER	Staffing grants: ~$90K per firefighter in years 1 – 2, ~$42K in year 3. Retention beyond grant period avoids full re-recruitment cycle.
QUALTRICS	Employee trends data collected from 2024 and 2025. New hire honeymoon period reversal; 39% of employees with less than six months tenure plan to leave within 12 months (2024); 27-point intent-to-stay gap between new hires and tenured employees (2025); employees under 25 are most engaged age group but have lowest three-year retention intent.

You are already paying for culture. The only question is whether you'll keep paying for the culture you have.

www.ingramcontent.com/pod-product-compliance
Lightning Source LLC
Chambersburg PA
CBHW071751150726
47998CB00005B/1898